Look, Learn & Create

Sewing

WORKSHOP
101
IN A BOOK

QUARRY

Inspiring | Educating | Creating | Entertaining

Brimming with creative inspiration, how-to projects, and useful information to enrich your everyday life, Quarto Knows is a favorite destination for those pursuing their interests and passions. Visit our site and dig deeper with our books into your area of interest: Quarto Creates, Quarto Cooks, Quarto Homes, Quarto Lives, Quarto Drives, Quarto Explores, Quarto Gifts, or Quarto Kids.

Library of Congress Cataloging-in-Publication Data

Sewing 101 / editors of Creative Publishing, International.
    p. cm.
  Includes index.
  ISBN-13: 978-1-58923-574-8 (soft cover)
  ISBN-10: 1-58923-574-6 (soft cover)
  1. Sewing--Amateurs' manuals. 2. Dressmaking--Amateurs' manuals. 3. Household linens. I. Creative Publishing International. II. Title: Sewing one hundred one. III. Title: Sewing one hundred and one.

  TT705.S465 2011
  646.4'04--dc22

                                        2010046930
Photo Coordinator: Joanne Wawra
Book Design and Layout: Mighty Media, Inc.
Illustrations: Heather Lambert
Videographer: Forrest Fox Productions
Video Script: Joanne Wawra

Printed in China

Videos of essential sewing techniques can be found at www.quartoknows.com/page/sewing101

CONTENTS

How to Use This Book

Welcome to the creative, sometimes challenging, but always rewarding world of sewing. Sewing 101 is designed to make your learning experience as painless as possible and to instill confidence as you take on new projects and learn new techniques. Easy-to-follow instructions with colorful photographs help you build your sewing skills while making clothes, gifts, and home decorating items that really appeal to you.

Sewing enthusiasts enjoy this time-honored art for a multitude of reasons. Those of us who came into this world as Baby Boomers may have begun sewing as adolescents wanting to ride the wave of trendy fashion while saving money over store-bought clothes. While this is not always the case today, sewing our own clothes still gives us the advantage of personalized fit and individual expression. Home decorating items are popular projects for beginners and advanced sewers alike, partly because of the cost savings over pur-

chased items. By sewing these items for the home, we also get to enjoy the creative fun of choosing styles, colors, and fabrics that fit our own personalities and tastes rather than those of the mass-produced market. But perhaps the greatest reason that sewing is so enjoyable is the mere satisfaction felt in creating something from scratch with your own two hands. Whether you are making something for yourself, your home, or to give to someone else, the ultimate reward is the intangible delight and personal fulfillment gained in the process.

The projects in this book are designed to guide you from your first nervous stitch at your sewing machine to comfortable familiarity. Each project will teach you new skills, listed under **What You'll Learn**. Throughout the book you will find tips and explanations to help you understand the "why" behind what you are doing. We also have included lots of variations for the projects, encouraging you to explore the unlimited design and fabric possibilities.

Use the first section of the book to acquaint yourself with your sewing machine and the techniques and supplies that encompass the art of sewing. Your sewing machine owner's manual is a necessity; refer to it first if you have questions or problems specific to your machine.

Quick reference text

Quick reference

The first step in any sewing project is to read through the directions from beginning to end. Refer to the **Quick Reference** for definitions or elaborations on any words or phrases printed *like this* on the page. If the word or phrase is followed by a page number, its reference can be found on the page indicated. At the beginning of every project you will find a list telling you **What You'll Need**. Read through the information on fabrics before you go shopping, so the fabric store will seem a little more user-friendly when you get there. Above all, enjoy the process. Give yourself the opportunity to be creative, and express yourself through the things you sew.

The online content associated with this book is an additional learning tool that will show you the essential techniques used for sewing. To access the online content, go to www.quartoknows.com/page/sewing101. Most of all, have fun with these sewing projects! Enjoy the creative process while you learn new skills.

Sewing Basics

There is no better place to start than at the very beginning. In writing this book, we assume you are starting from scratch, and we know that for a new sewer, even a trip to the fabric store can be challenging. Manufacturers can't include all the vital information with their packaging, and there are so many tools and sewing notions to choose from. To give you a firm foundation for learning to sew, this section teaches you the essentials about your sewing machine, fabrics, patterns, and sewing supplies. If you have never taken a stitch, you will appreciate the detailed information, photos, and illustrations. Even if you have a little sewing experience, you are sure to learn some things you didn't know. So settle back, take your time, and jump into the basics.

The Sewing Machine

The principle parts common to all modern sewing machines are shown in the diagram at right. The parts may look different on your model, and they may have slightly different locations, so open your owner's manual, also. If you do not have an owner's manual for your machine, you should be able to get one from a sewing machine dealer who sells your brand. Become familiar with the names of the parts and their functions. As you spend more time sewing, these items will become second nature to you.

If you are buying a new machine, consider how much and what kind of sewing you expect to do. Talk to friends who sew and to sales personnel. Ask for demonstrations, and sew on the machine yourself. Experiment with the various features while sewing on a variety of fabrics, including knits, wovens, light-weights, and denim. Think about the optional features of the machine and which ones you want on yours. Many dealers offer free sewing lessons with the purchase of a machine. Take advantage! These lessons will be geared to your particular brand and model of sewing machine.

These parts are common to all sewing machines, but their position and design differs. Use your manual to help you learn where these parts are, what these parts do, and how to use them:

Bobbin
Bobbin case
Bobbin winder spindle
Bobbin winder tension
Buttonhole knob
Detachable machine bed
Feed dogs
Feed dog control
General-purpose presser foot
Handwheel
Light switch
Needle clamp
Presser foot lifter

Presser foot pressure control
Spool pins
Stitch pattern selector
Stitch length selector
Stitch width selector
Take-up lever
Top tension control
Top tension discs
Thread cutter
Thread guides
Throat plate
Variable speed switch

Machine Accessories

Sewing Machine Needles

Sewing machine needles come in a variety of styles and sizes. The correct needle choice depends mostly on the fabric you have selected. Sharp points (A), used for woven fabrics, are designed to pierce the fabric. Ballpoints (B) are designed to slip between the loops of knit fabric rather than pierce and possibly damage the fabric. Universal points are designed to work on both woven and knitted fabrics. The size of the needle is designated by a number, generally given in both European (60, 70, 80, 90, 100, 110) and American (9, 11, 12, 14, 16, 18) numbering systems. Use size 11/70 or 12/80 needles for medium-weight fabrics. A larger number means the needle is thicker and that it is appropriate for use with heavier fabrics and heavier threads.

Bobbins

Stitches are made by locking the upper thread with a lower thread, carried on a bobbin. Always use bobbins in the correct style and size for your machine. Bobbin thread tension is controlled by a spring on the bobbin case, which may be built in (C) or removable (D).

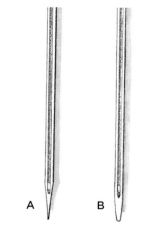

A   B

TIP Though needle style and size are usually indicated in some way on the needle, it is often difficult to see without a magnifying glass, and you most likely will not remember what needle is in the machine. As an easy reminder, when you finish a sewing session, leave a fabric swatch from your current project under the presser foot.

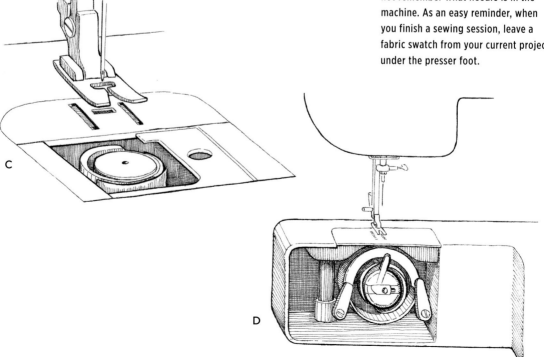

C

D

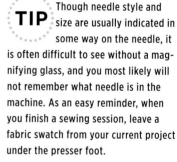

Presser Feet

Every sewing machine comes with accessories for specialized tasks. More can be purchased as you develop your interest and skills. Your machine manual or dealer can show you what accessories are available and will explain how to use them to get the best results.

A general-purpose foot (A), probably the one you will use most often, has a wide opening to accommodate the side-to-side movement of the needle in all types of utility (nondecorative) stitches. It is also suitable for most straight stitching. A zipper foot (B) is used to insert zippers or to stitch any seam that has more bulk on one side than the other. For some sewing machines, the zipper foot is stationary, requiring you to move the needle position to the right or left. For other styles, the position of the zipper foot itself is adjustable. A special-purpose or embroidery foot (C) has a grooved bottom that allows the foot to ride smoothly over decorative stitches or raised cords. Some styles are clear plastic, allowing you to see your work more clearly. A walking foot (D) feeds top and bottom layers at equal rates, allowing you to more easily match patterns or stitch bulky layers.

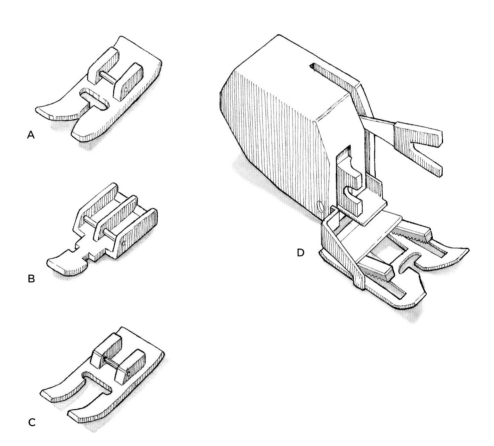

A

B

C

D

Getting Ready to Sew

Simple tasks of inserting the needle, winding the bobbin, and threading the machine have tremendous influence on the stitch quality and performance of your machine. Use this guide as a general reference, but refer to your owner's manual for instructions specific to your machine.

Inserting the Needle

Loosen the needle clamp. After selecting the appropriate needle for your project (page 10), insert it into the machine as high as it will go. The grooved side of the needle faces forward, if your bobbin gets inserted from the front or top; it faces to the left, if your bobbin gets inserted on the left. Tighten the clamp securely.

Winding the Bobbin

If the bobbin case is built in, the bobbin is wound in place with the machine fully threaded as if to sew (page 14).

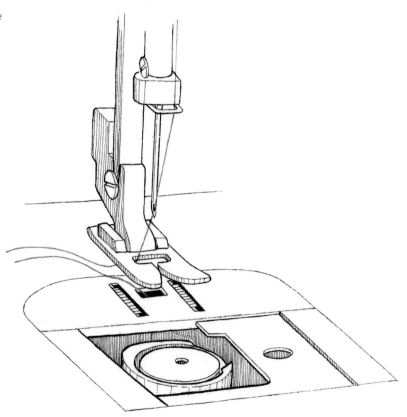

Removable bobbins are wound on the top or side of the machine, with the machine threaded for bobbin winding, as described in your owner's manual.

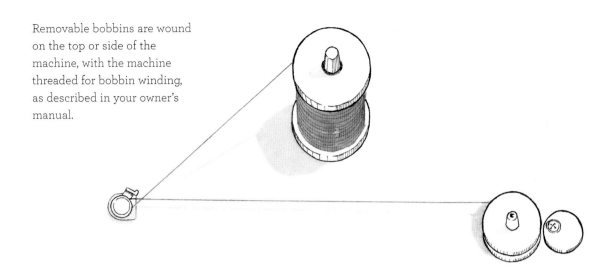

Bobbin thread must be drawn through the bobbin case tension spring. For wind-in-place bobbins, this happens automatically when you wind the bobbin, but you must do it manually when you insert a bobbin that already has thread on it.

After inserting the bobbin and threading the machine (page 14), you need to draw the bobbin thread to the top. Hold the needle thread while turning the handwheel toward you one full turn. As the needle goes down, the top thread interlocks with the bobbin thread and brings it up through the needle hole. Pull both threads together under the presser foot and off to the side or back.

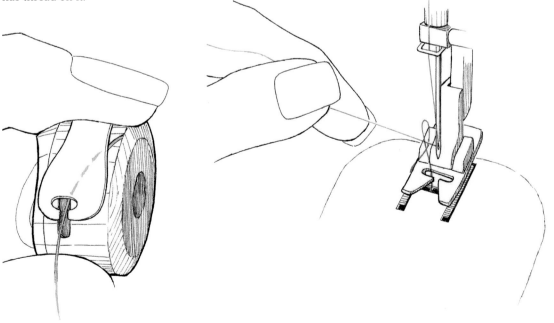

Threading the Machine

Because every sewing machine is different, the threading procedure for your machine may differ slightly from the one shown here. Once again, it is important to refer to your owner's manual. Every upper thread guide adds a little tension to the thread as it winds its way to the needle. Missing one of them can make a big difference in the quality of your stitches.

1 Set the thread spool on the spindle. For a vertical spindle, position the spool so that it will turn clockwise as you sew. If the spindle is horizontal, the spool is held in place with an end cap. If your spool has a small cut in one end for minding the thread, position the spool with that end to the right.

TIP If the spool is new and has paper labels covering the holes, poke them in, completely uncovering the holes, to allow the spool to turn freely.

Unless your machine has a self-winding bobbin, you will want to wind the bobbin (page 13) before threading the machine.

2 Pull thread to the left and through the first thread guide.

3 Draw thread through the tension guide.

4 Draw thread through the next thread guide.

5 Insert thread through the take-up lever.

6 Draw the thread through the remaining thread guides.

7 Thread the needle. Most needles are threaded from front to back; some, from left to right.

TIP It is very important to have the presser foot lever up when threading the machine because the tension discs are then open. If the presser foot is down and the discs are closed, the thread will not slide between the discs, and your stitches will not make you happy.

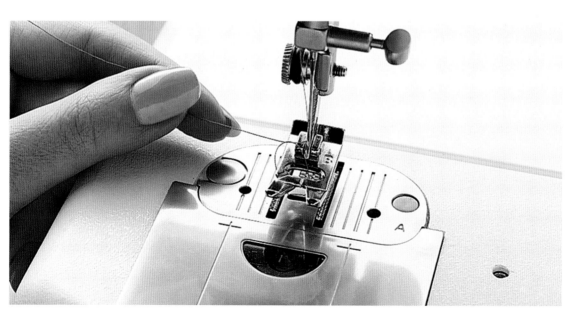

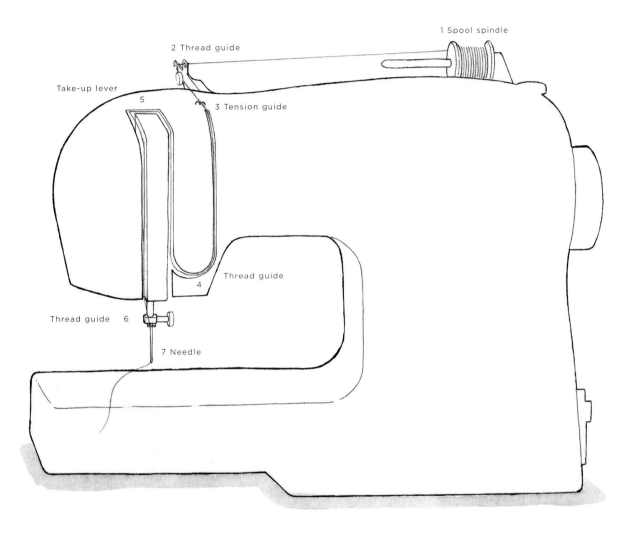

1 Spool spindle

2 Thread guide

Take-up lever

5

3 Tension guide

4 Thread guide

Thread guide   6

7 Needle

How to Balance Tension

Your machine forms stitches by interlocking the bobbin thread with the needle thread. Every time the needle goes down into the fabric, a sharp hook catches the needle thread and wraps the bobbin thread around it. Imagine this little tug-of-war. If the needle thread tension is "stronger" than the bobbin thread tension, the needle thread pulls the bobbin thread through to the top. If the bobbin thread tension is "stronger," it pulls the needle thread through to the bottom. When the tensions are evenly balanced, the stitch will lock exactly halfway between the top and bottom of the layers being sewn, which is right where you want it.

Some machines have "self-adjusting tension," meaning the machine automatically adjusts its tension with every fabric you sew. For machines that do not have this feature, you may have to adjust the needle thread tension slightly as you sew different fabrics.

1 Thread your machine and insert the bobbin, using two very different colors of thread, neither of which matches the fabric. Cut an 8" (20.5 cm) square of a smooth, mediumweight fabric. Fold the fabric in half diagonally, and place it under the presser foot so the fold aligns to your ½" (1.3 cm) seam guide. Lower the presser foot and set your stitch length at ten stitches per inch or 2.5 mm long.

2 Stitch a line across the fabric, stitching ½" (1.3 cm) from the diagonal fold. Remove the fabric from the machine. Inspect your stitching line from both sides. If your tension is evenly balanced, you will see only one color on each side. If you see both thread colors on the top side of your sample, the needle tension is tighter than the bobbin tension. If you see both thread colors on the back side of your sample, the bobbin tension is tighter than the needle tension.

3 Pull on your stitching line until you hear threads break. (Because you stitched on the BIAS, the fabric will stretch slightly.) If the thread breaks on only one side, your machine's tension is tighter on that side.

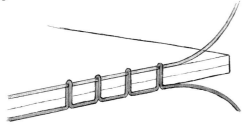

Top tension too tight

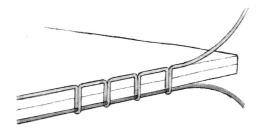

Top tension too loose

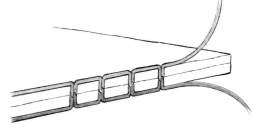

Tensions even

Adjusting the Tension

Before adjusting the tension on your machine, first check:

- that your machine is properly threaded (page 14)
- that your bobbin is properly installed
- that your needle is not damaged and is inserted correctly

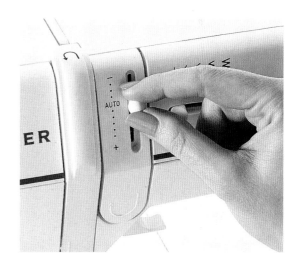

After checking these three things, you may need to adjust the tension on your machine. (Check your owner's manual.) Tighten or loosen the needle thread tension slightly to bring the needle thread and bobbin thread tensions into balance. Test the stitches after each adjustment, until you achieve balanced tension. If slight adjustments of the needle tension dial do not solve the problem, the bobbin tension may need adjusting. However, most manufacturers do not recommend that you adjust bobbin tension yourself, so unless you have received instructions for adjusting the bobbin tension on your machine, take your machine in for repair.

Sewing a Seam

You may or may not be familiar with the very basic technique of running your machine and sewing a seam. Use this exercise as a refresher course whenever you feel you have lost touch with the basics or if your personal technique has become sloppy. Little frustrations, such as thread jams, erratic stitching lines, or having the thread pull out of the needle at the start of a seam, can often be prevented or corrected by following these basic guidelines. If you are really not sure where to begin, then you should probably begin right here!

How to Sew a Seam

1 Thread your machine (page 14) and insert the bobbin (page 13). Holding the needle thread with your left hand, turn the handwheel toward you until the needle has gone down and come back up to its highest point. A stitch will form, and you will feel a tug on the needle thread. Pull on the needle thread to bring the bobbin thread up through the hole in the throat plate. Pull both threads together under the presser foot and off to one side.

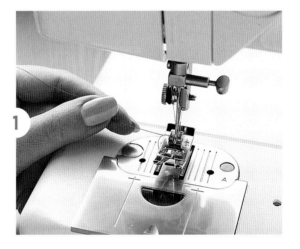

2 Cut rectangles of mediumweight fabric. Place the pieces right sides together, aligning the outer edges. Pin the pieces together along one long edge, **inserting the pins** about every 2" (5 cm), **perpendicular to the edge**. Place the fabric under the presser foot so the pinned side edges align to the ½" (1.3 cm) **seam allowance guide** and the upper edges align to the back of the presser foot. Lower the presser foot, and set your stitch length at 2.5 mm, which equals 10 stitches per inch.

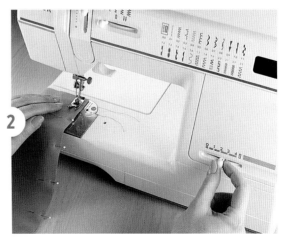

3 Begin by **backstitching** several stitches to the upper edge of the fabric. Hold the thread tails under a finger for the first few stitches. This prevents the needle thread from being pulled out of the needle and also prevents the thread tails from being drawn down into the bobbin case, where they could potentially cause the dreaded thread jam.

4 Stitch forward over the backstitched line, and continue sewing the ½" (1.3 cm) seam. Gently guide the fabric while you sew by walking your fingers ahead of and slightly to the sides of the presser foot. Remember, you are only guiding; let the machine pull the fabric.

5 Stop stitching and **remove pins as you come to them**. When you reach the end of the fabric, stop stitching; backstitch several stitches, and stop again. Turn the handwheel toward you until the needle is in its highest position.

6 Raise the presser foot. Pull the fabric smoothly away from the presser foot, either to the left side or straight back. If you have to tug the threads, turn your handwheel slightly toward you until they pull easily. Cut the threads, leaving tails 2½" to 3" (6.5 to 7.5 cm) long.

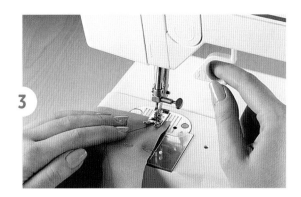

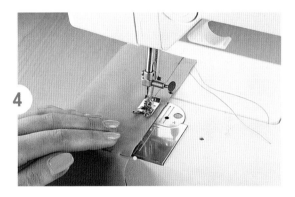

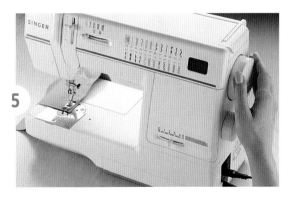

QUICK REFERENCE

Inserting the pins perpendicular to the edge. This makes it much easier to remove them as you sew, The pin heads are near the raw edge where you can easily grasp them with your right hand. In this position, you are much less likely to stick yourself with a pin as you sew.

Seam allowance guide. Most machines have a series of lines on the throat plate. These lines mark the distance from the needle (where a standard straight stitch seam would be) to the cut edges. Measure these lines on your machine to determine where the edge of your fabric should be for the width seam you are stitching.

Backstitching secures the beginning and end of your stitching line so that the stitches will not pull out. The method for backstitching varies with each sewing machine. You may need to lift and hold your stitch length lever, push in and hold a button, or simply touch an icon. Check your owner's manual.

Remove pins as you come to them. As tempting as it may be, don't sew over pins! You may be lucky and save a few seconds, or you could hit a pin and break your needle, costing you much more time in the long run.

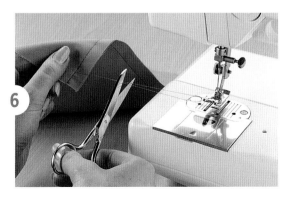

Special Seams

Aside from the standard straight-stitch seam, your machine is probably capable of sewing several other stitches that are appropriate for various fabrics and situations. Whenever you sew with knits, for example, you want a seam that will stretch with the fabric. To prevent raveling of woven fabrics, seam allowance edges must be finished. There are several finishing methods to choose from, depending on the fabric and the capabilities of your machine. These general guidelines will help you decide when to use these stitches and finishing methods. Your owner's manual is the best source of specific information for your machine.

Stretch Seams

Double-stitched seam. Stitch on the seamline, using a straight stitch set at a length of 12 stitches per inch, which equals 2 mm long. Stretch the fabric slightly as you sew, to allow the finished seam to stretch that much. Stitch again ⅛" (3 mm) into the seam allowance. Trim the seam allowance close to the second stitching line. This seam is appropriate for fabrics with minimal stretch or for seams sewn in the vertical direction on moderate stretch knits.

Narrow zigzag seam. Stitch on the seamline, using a very narrow zigzag stitch set at 12 stitches per inch, which equals 2 mm long. If the fabric is very stretchy in the direction you are sewing, you may also stretch the fabric slightly as you sew. Trim the seam allowance to ¼" (6 mm), if necessary. Set the zigzag wider, and stitch the seam allowance edges together. This seam is appropriate for very stretchy knits.

Built-in stretch stitch. Differing from brand to brand, these stitches are designed to incorporate stretch, so that you do not need to stretch the fabric as you sew. Some stitch styles, like the bottom two samples, are a pattern of zigzag and straight stitches that stitch and finish the seam in one pass. Check your manual for stitch settings.

TIP The cut edges of knit fabrics do not ravel, but they often curl. To minimize this problem, the seam allowances are usually finished together and pressed to one side.

Seam Finishes

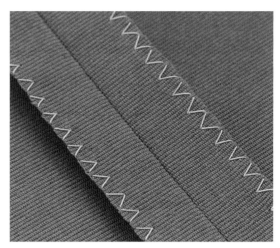

Stitched and pinked finish. Stitch ¼" (6 mm) from each seam allowance edge, using a straight stitch set at 12 stitches per inch, which equals 2 mm. Trim close to the stitching, using pinking shears (page 29). This finish is suitable for finely woven fabrics that do not ravel easily.

Zigzag finish. Set the zigzag stitch on or near maximum width and a length of 10 stitches per inch, which equals 2.5 mm. Stitch close to the edge of each seam allowance so that the right-hand stitches go just over the edge. If the fabric puckers, try a narrower zigzag width.

Multistitch-zigzag finish. If your machine has this stitch, check your owner's manual for directions on selecting the settings. Stitch near, but not over the edge of, each seam allowance.

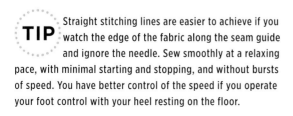

TIP Straight stitching lines are easier to achieve if you watch the edge of the fabric along the seam guide and ignore the needle. Sew smoothly at a relaxing pace, with minimal starting and stopping, and without bursts of speed. You have better control of the speed if you operate your foot control with your heel resting on the floor.

Turn and zigzag finish. Set the zigzag stitch near maximum width at a length of 10 stitches per inch, which equals 2.5 mm. Turn under the seam allowance edge ⅛" to ¼" (3 to 6 mm). Stitch close to the folded edge so that the right-hand stitches go just on or over the fold. Use this finish on loosely woven fabrics, especially on garments, such as jackets, where the inside may be visible occasionally.

Hand Stitches

While modern sewers rely on sewing machines for speedy construction, there are situations when hand stitching is necessary or preferable. You may need to slipstitch an opening closed to finish a pillow, or perhaps you like the look of a hand-stitched blind hem (page 24) on a skirt. Of course you'll also need to sew on buttons.

Threading the Needle

Insert the thread end through the needle's eye, for sewing with a single strand. Or fold the thread in half, and insert the fold through the eye, for sewing with a double strand. Pull through about 8" (20.5 cm). Wrap the other end(s) around your index finger. Then, using your thumb, roll the thread off your finger, twisting it into a knot.

TIP Use a single strand when slipstitching or hemming. Use a double strand when sewing on buttons. To avoid tangles, begin with thread no longer than 18" (46 cm) from the needle to the knot. Run the thread through beeswax (page 27), if desired.

Slipstitching

1 Insert the threaded needle between the seam allowance and the garment, just behind the opening. Bring it to the outside in the seamline. If you are right-handed, work from right to left; lefties work from left to right.

2 Insert the needle into the fold just behind where the thread came up, and run it inside the fold for about ¼" (6 mm). Bring the needle out, and draw the thread snug. Take your next stitch in the opposite fold, inserting the needle directly across from the previous stitch.

3 Continue, crossing from one fold to the other, until you have sewn past the opening. Secure the thread with several tiny stitches in the seamline. Then take a long stitch, and pull it tight. Clip the thread at the surface, and let the tail disappear inside.

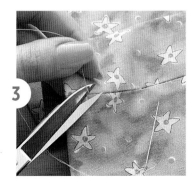

Sewing on a Shank Button

1 Place the button on the mark, with the shank hole parallel to the buttonhole. Secure the thread on the right side of the garment with a small stitch under the button.

2 Bring the needle through the shank hole. Insert the needle down through the fabric and pull the thread through. Take four to six stitches in this manner.

3 Secure the thread in the fabric under the button by making a knot or by taking several small stitches. Clip the thread ends.

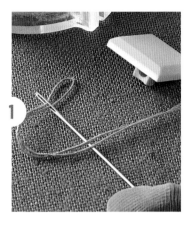

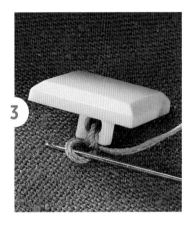

Sewing on a Sew-through Button

1 Place the button on the mark, with the holes lining up parallel to the buttonhole. Bring the needle through the fabric from the underside and up through one hole in the button. Insert the needle into another hole and through the fabric layers.

2 Slip a toothpick, match, or sewing machine needle between the thread and the button to form a shank. Take three or four stitches through each pair of holes. Bring the needle and thread to the right side under the button. Remove the toothpick.

3 Wind the thread two or three times around the button stitches to form the shank. Secure the thread on the right side under the button, by making a knot or taking several small stitches. Clip the threads close to the knot.

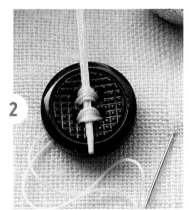

Hems

There are a number of ways to hem the lower edges of skirts, pants, jackets, and shirts. Some hems are sewn by machine; others by hand. The method you choose will depend on the fabric, the garment style, and your own preference. For methods that do not involve turning under the raw edge, finish the edge (page 21) in an appropriate manner, before hemming.

Hand Hems

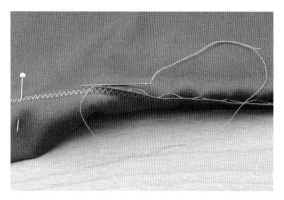

Blindstitch. Fold back the finished edge of the hem ¼" (6 mm). Take a small stitch to anchor the thread in a seam allowance. Work with the needle pointing in the direction you are going. Take a very small horizontal stitch in the garment, catching only one or two threads. Take the next stitch in the hem, ¼" to ½" (6 mm to 1.3 cm) away from the first stitch. Continue alternating stitches; do not pull too tightly.

Blind catchstitch. Fold back the finished edge of the hem ¼" (6 mm). Take a small stitch to anchor the thread in a seam allowance. Work with the needle pointing in the direction opposite from the way you are going. Take a very small horizontal stitch in the garment, catching only one or two threads. Take the next stitch in the hem, ¼" to ½" (6 mm to 1.3 cm) away from the first stitch, crossing the stitches. Continue alternating the stitches in a zigzag pattern.

Slipstitch. Fold under the raw edge ¼" (6 mm), and press. Take a small stitch to anchor the thread in a seam allowance. Work with the needle pointing in the direction you are going. Follow the directions for slipstitching on page 22, catching only one or two threads with each stitch that goes into the garment.

Machine Hems

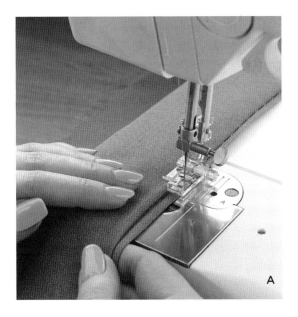

Double-fold hem. This method results in one or two rows of straight stitches showing on the right side. Follow page 98, step 9 to press the hem folds. Then stitch along the inner fold and repeat at the outer fold, if desired. This method is most successful on straight edges where there is no excess fullness to ease in.

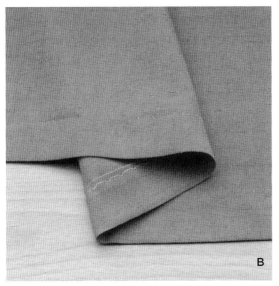

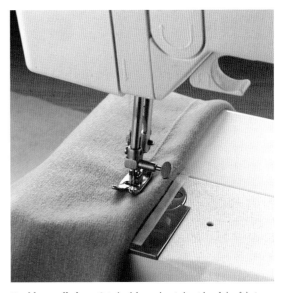

Machine blindstitch. Follow your manual for adjusting the stitch settings, and use the appropriate presser foot. Test the stitch on a scrap of the garment fabric until you are happy with the results. (A) Place the hem allowance facedown on the machine bed, with the bulk of the garment folded back. Allow about ¼" (6 mm) of the hem edge to extend under the presser foot, aligning the soft fold to rest against the guide in the foot. Stitch along the hem, close to the fold, catching only one or two threads of the garment with each left-hand stitch of the needle. (B) When complete, open out the hem, and press it flat.

Double-needle hem. Stitched from the right side of the fabric, this hem is suitable for knit garments, because it will stretch slightly. The farther apart the needles are spaced, the more stretch the hem will have. However, widely spaced needles will usually produce a ridge between the stitching lines. Using two thread spools on top, thread both needles. Place tape on the bed of the machine as a stitching guide.

Sewing Supplies

Sewing involves many steps: measuring, laying out the pattern, cutting, marking, stitching, and pressing. For each of these steps there are special tools and supplies to make your sewing easier and help you complete your projects successfully. Don't feel you need to buy all the items before you start. For instance, a pair of sharp shears and a seam ripper will see you through most of the cutting tasks for the projects in this book. You will undoubtedly acquire additional tools as your skills and interests grow.

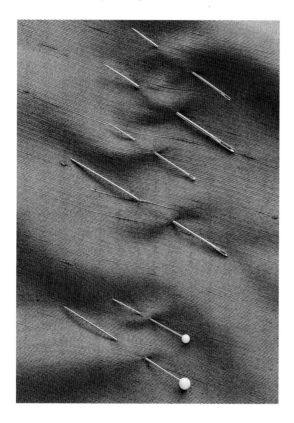

Hand-sewing Supplies

Needles and pins are available in a variety of sizes and styles. Look for rustproof needles and pins made of brass, nickel-plated steel, or stainless steel. Pictured from top to bottom:

Sharps are all-purpose, medium-length needles designed for general sewing.

Crewels are sharp, large-eyed medium-length needles, designed for embroidery.

Betweens are very short and round-eyed. They are useful for hand quilting and making fine stitches.

Milliner's needles are long with round eyes and are used for making long basting or gathering stitches.

Straight pins are used for general sewing. They should be slim and are usually $1\frac{1}{16}$" (2.7 cm) long. Pins with colored ball heads are easier to see and are less likely to get lost than those with flat heads.

Quilting pins are $1\frac{3}{4}$" (4.5 cm) long. Their extra length makes them ideal for use on bulky fabrics or fabrics with extra loft.

A thimble (A) protects your finger while hand sewing. Available in a variety of styles and sizes, it is worn on whichever finger you use to push the needle through the fabric. Most people prefer either the middle or ring finger. Using a thimble is an acquired habit. Some people can't get along without one, while others feel they are a nuisance.

Pincushions (B) provide a safe and handy place to store pins. One style is worn on the wrist for convenience. Another style, a magnetic tray, attracts and holds steel pins. Be careful not to place any magnetic tools near a computerized machine, because the magnet may interfere with the machine's memory.

Needle threaders (C) ease threading of hand and machine needles. This is especially useful if you have difficulty seeing something that small.

Thread can be drawn through beeswax (D) to strengthen it and prevent it from tangling while hand sewing.

Measuring & Marking Tools

(A) Transparent ruler allows you to see what you are measuring and marking. It also is used to check fabric grainline.

(B) Yardstick (meterstick) should be made of smooth hardwood or metal.

(C) Tape measure has the flexibility helpful for measuring items with shape and dimension. Select one made of a material that will not stretch.

(D) Seam gauge is a 6" (15 cm) metal or plastic ruler with a sliding marker. It helps take quick, accurate measurements and can be used to measure seam allowance widths.

(E) Transparent T-square is used to locate grainline and to measure 90-degree angles.

(F) Marking chalk is available in several forms: as powder in a rolling wheel dispenser, as a pencil, or as a flat slice. Chalk lines are easily removable from most fabrics.

(G) Fabric marking pens are available in both air-erasable and water-erasable forms. Air-erasable marks disappear within 48 hours; water-erasable marks wash off with a sprinkling of water.

(H) Narrow masking tape is an alternative method for marking fabrics when other methods are less suitable.

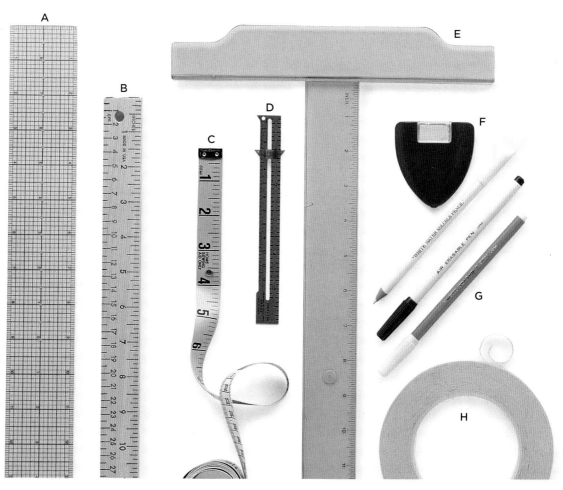

Cutting Tools

Buy quality cutting tools and use them only for your sewing! Cutting paper or other household materials will dull your cutting tools quickly. Dull tools are not only tiresome to work with, they can also damage fabric. Scissors have both handles the same size; shears have one handle larger than the other. The best-quality scissors and shears are hot-forged, high-grade steel, honed to a fine cutting edge. Have your cutting tools sharpened periodically by a qualified professional.

(I) Bent-handled dressmaker's shears are best for cutting out garment pieces because the angle of the lower blade lets fabric lie flat on the cutting surface. Blade lengths of 7" or 8" (18 or 20.5 cm) are most popular, but lengths of up to 12" (30.5 cm) are available. Select a blade length appropriate for the size of your hand; shorter lengths for smaller hands. Left-handed models are also available. If you intend to sew a great deal, invest in a pair of all-steel, chrome-plated shears for heavy-duty cutting. Lighter models with stainless steel blades and plastic handles are fine for less-frequent sewing or lightweight fabrics.

(J) Sewing scissors with pointed tips are handy for clipping threads and trimming and clipping seam allowances. A 6" (15 cm) blade is suitable for most tasks.

(K) Seam ripper quickly removes stitches and opens buttonholes. Use it carefully to avoid cutting the fabric.

(L) Rotary cutter works like a pizza cutter and can be used by left-handed or right-handed sewers. A locking mechanism retracts the blade for safety. Use the rotary cutter with a special plastic mat, available in different sizes, with or without grid lines. The self-healing mat protects both the work surface and the blade.

(M) Pinking shears and pinking rotary cutters are used to finish seams. They cut fabric in a zigzag or scalloped pattern instead of a straight line.

Pressing Tools

Pressing at each stage of construction is the secret to a perfectly finished garment. The general rule is to press each stitched seam before crossing it with another.

(A) Steam/spray iron should have a wide temperature range to accommodate all fabrics. Buy a dependable, name-brand iron. An iron that steams and sprays at any setting, not just the higher heat settings, is helpful for fabrics with synthetic fibers.

(B) Press cloth helps prevent iron shine and is always used when applying fusibles. The transparent cloth allows you to see if the fabric is smooth and the layers are properly aligned.

(C) Teflon-coated sole plate guard, available to fit most irons, eliminates the need for a press cloth.

(D) Seam roll is a firmly packed cylindrical cushion for pressing seams. The bulk of the fabric falls to the sides away from the iron, preventing the seam from making an imprint on the right side of the fabric.

(E) Pressing ham is a firmly packed cushion for pressing curved areas of a garment.

(F) Sleeve board looks like two small ironing boards attached one on top of the other. It is useful for pressing sleeves one layer at a time to avoid unwanted creases.

Special Products

Many special products and gadgets are designed to assist you in various steps of the sewing process. Before using a new product, read the manufacturer's instructions carefully. Learn what special handling or care is required, and for what fabrics or sewing techniques it is especially suited. Here are some specialized products that you may find helpful in sewing your clothes, accessories, or home décor items.

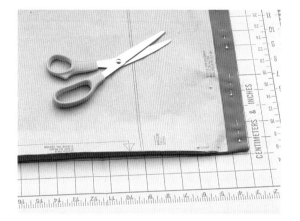

Cutting boards protect table finished from scratches. Available in cardboard, plastic, or padded styles, these boards also hold fabric more securely while cutting. Square off fabric using the marked lines, and use the 1" (2.5 cm) squares as an instant measure.

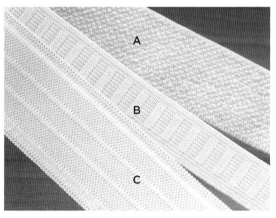

Elastics can be purchased in a variety of widths and styles, either in precut packages or by the yard (meter). Softer elastics (A) are suitable for pajamas or boxer shorts; nonroll elastic (B) stays flat in the casing; some wide elastic has channels for topstitching (C).

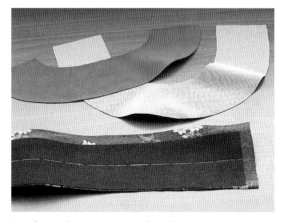

Interfacing plays a supporting role in almost every garment. It is an inner layer of fabric, used to stabilize the fabric in areas like necklines and waist-bands, or give support behind buttons and buttonholes. Interfacings may be woven, nonwoven, or knit; the easiest forms to use are heat fusible.

A bodkin is used to thread elastic or cording through a casing. One end holds the elastic tightly while you feed the tool through the narrow casing, pulling the elastic or cording behind it.

Point turner is helpful for perfecting corners, such as at the top of a pocket or at the ends of a waistband, or inside a pillow cover. Slip the tool inside the item, and gently poke the fabric out into a point.

Liquid fray preventer is a colorless plastic liquid that prevents fraying by stiffening the fabric slightly. It is helpful when you have clipped too far into a seam allowance or want to reinforce a buttonhole. It may discolor some fabrics, so test before using, and apply carefully. The liquid may be removed with rubbing alcohol. It dries to a permanent finish that will withstand laundering and dry cleaning.

Glue stick is a convenient substitute for pinning or basting when you need to hold an item in place temporarily before stitching. The temporary adhesive in a retractable tube can be applied in small dots. It won't discolor the fabric and washed out completely, if necessary. It will not harm your machine or gum up your needle as you stitch through it.

Buttonhole cutter is a handy tool for making precision cuts down the center of buttonholes. It comes with a wooden block to place under the fabric to protect your work surface and accept the sharp thin blade of the cutter. While buttonholes can be cut open with small scissors or a seam ripper, a buttonhole cutter is more accurate and less likely to cut the stitches.

(continued)

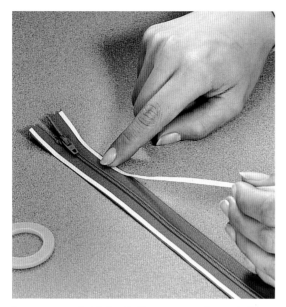

Basting tape is double-faced adhesive tape used instead of pinning or basting. It is especially helpful for matching prints, applying zippers, and positioning trims. Some manufacturers advise that you avoid stitching through the tape because the adhesive may collect on your needle.

Single-fold bias tape is useful for hemming curved edges, such as a round tablecloth. The manufacturer has already cut the bias strips, sewn them together, and pressed in precise folds to make your sewing easier. The tape is available in packaged lengths in a wide ranges of colors.

Paper-backed fusible web is sold on rolls, in various narrow widths. It is also available as a wide sheet rolled on a bolt for purchase by the yard (meter). It is a time-saving product used for adhering two pieces of fabric together. For instance, you may use narrow strips of it to secure the side hems of a Roman shade instead of stitching them. A protective paper backing is removed from one side after the other side has been fused to the fabric.

Blanket binding resembles a wide satin ribbon that has been pressed in half for encasing the raw edge around a blanket. Packaged in a convenient length for sewing baby blankets, the binding is available in assorted soft colors and white. Because of its stability and permanent crease, it is easy to work with, yet feels silky smooth against a baby's skin.

Welting is a fabric-covered cording sewn into a seam or around an outer edge to provide extra strength and a decorative finishing touch. It is available in many colors and various diameters to purchase by the yard (meter) or in precut packaged lengths.

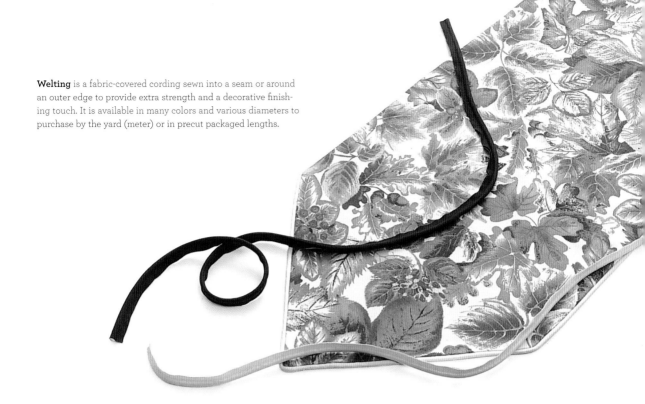

Batting. Low-loft cotton, polyester, or poly/cotton blend batting, sold in packages, is used for quilted projects, such as channel-quilted placemats. It is soft and drapable.

Fabric Information

Selecting the right fabrics for your projects may seem like an overwhelming task, but there are a few simple guidelines to help narrow the field. One good way to learn about fabrics is to browse through a fabric store, handling the fabrics and reading the fiber content information and care instructions printed on the ends of the bolts. You may already know whether you want a solid color, a printed pattern, or perhaps a multicolored fabric. Do you need a fabric that can be laundered frequently? Do you want smooth or textured, stiff or drapable, lightweight or heavy? Some basic fabric knowledge and a thought-out plan will help you make wise choices and avoid costly errors.

Fiber Content

Natural fabrics are made from plant or animal fibers, spun into yarns: cotton, wool, silk, and linen are most common. Naturals are often considered the easiest fabrics to sew. Synthetic fabrics, made from chemically produced fibers, include nylon, acrylic, acetate, and polyester. Rayon is a man-made fiber made from a plant source. Each fiber has unique characteristics, desirable for different reasons. Many fabrics are a blend of natural and synthetic fibers, offering you the best qualities of each, such as the breathable comfort of cotton blended with the wrinkle resistance of polyester.

Cotton print

Wool melton

Linen

Dupioni silk

Woven acrylic

Acetate

Polyester

Rayon velvet

Crinkled nylon

Synthetic fabrics are made to resemble the look and feel of natural fabrics. Polyester may look like cotton or silk, acetate and nylon shimmer like silk, and acrylic mimics the texture and appearance of wool.

Woven Fabrics

Woven fabrics have straight lengthwise and crosswise yarns. The pattern in which the yarns are woven gives the fabric its characteristic surface texture and appearance. The outer edges of woven fabrics are called selvages. As a general rule, they should be trimmed away because they are often heavier than the rest of the fabric, and they may shrink when laundered or pressed. Grainlines are the directions in which the fabric yarns run. Strong, stable lengthwise yarns, running parallel to the selvages, form the lengthwise grain. The crosswise grain is perpendicular to the lengthwise grain and has a small amount of give. Any diagonal direction, called the bias, has a fair amount of stretch.

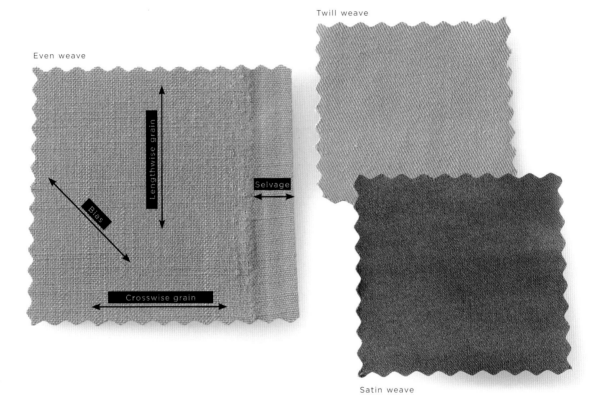

Even weave

Lengthwise grain

Bias

Selvage

Crosswise grain

Twill weave

Satin weave

Knit Fabrics

Knit fabrics consist of rows of interlocking loops of yarn, as in a hand-knit sweater, but usually on a finer scale. Knit fabrics are more flexible than other fabrics, and they all stretch. These features mean that garments made of knits require less fitting and offer more freedom of movement. When sewing with knits, select patterns that are specifically designed for knit fabrics.

Knit fabric is made from interlocking looped stitches. The lengthwise rows of stitches are called ribs; the crosswise rows are called courses. These ribs and courses correspond to the lengthwise and crosswise grains of woven fabrics.

Patterns designed for knit fabrics have a stretch gauge. Fold over the fabric along a crosswise course several inches (centimeters) from a cut end, and test its degree of stretch against the gauge. If the fabric stretches the necessary amount without distortion, it is suitable for the pattern.

Stretch terry

Synthetic fleece

Double knit

Sweatshirt fleece

Novelty knit

Moiré

Jacquard

Cotton sateen
print

Twill weave
(top right)

Cotton sateen

Novelty weave

Decorator Fabrics

Fabric Shopping

Fabrics in a store are divided into fashion fabrics and decorator fabrics. Decorator fabrics are generally more durable than fashion fabrics; most have stain-resistant finishes. They are designed for pillows, slip-covers, window treatments, and other home decorating projects. They are manufactured in widths (cross-wise grain) of 48" or 54" (122 or 137 cm), though occasionally you may find some wider. To prevent creases, decorator fabrics are rolled on tubes.

Fashion fabrics are usually folded double and rolled on cardboard bolts. They vary in width; the most common are 36", 45", and 60" (91.5, 115, and 152.5 cm). Though fashion fabrics are intended for apparel, many of them are also suitable for home decorating. Most stores arrange their fashion fabrics according to the fiber content or fabric style. For example, all the wools and wool blends, suitable for skirts, slacks, and jackets, may be found together in one area of the store; all the bridal and special-occasion fabrics located in another area; quilting fabrics (lightweight cottons) in another. This is not a hard-and-fast rule, however, so you will want to spend time getting acquainted with the fabric stores you shop.

Fabric Preparation

Preshrink washable fabric before cutting out the project, by washing and drying it in the same way you will care for the finished item. Because most decorator fabrics are not washable and require dry cleaning when necessary, preshrink them by pressing with steam, moving the iron evenly along the grainlines. Allow the fabric to dry before moving it.

Cotton corduroy

Silk

Polyester fleece

Cotton denim

Fashion Fabrics

Linen

Cutting Decorator Fabrics

Cutting into a new piece of fabric may seem a little scary, considering the investment you have just made. Here are a few guidelines for accurate cutting that should boost your confidence.

After preshrinking, straighten the cut ends of the fabric, using one of the three methods opposite. Then mark the other cutting lines, using the straightened edge as a guide. Before cutting full-width pieces of fabric for large home décor projects, such as tablecloths, duvet covers, or Roman shades, pin-mark the placement of each cut along the selvage. Mark out pieces for smaller projects, like decorator pillows or napkins, with chalk. Double-check your measurements and inspect the fabric for flaws. Once you have cut into the fabric, you cannot return it. To ensure that large décor items will hang or lay straight, the fabric lengths must be cut on-grain. This means that the cuts are made along the exact crosswise grain of the fabric. Patterned decorator fabrics are cut following the pattern repeat rather than the grainline so they must be **printed on-grain**.

For tightly woven fabrics without a matchable pattern, mark straight cuts on the crosswise grain, using a carpenter's square. Align one edge to a selvage and mark along the perpendicular side.

For loosely woven fabrics, such as linen tablecloth fabric, pull out a yarn along the crosswise grain, from selvage to selvage. Cut along the line left by the missing yarn.

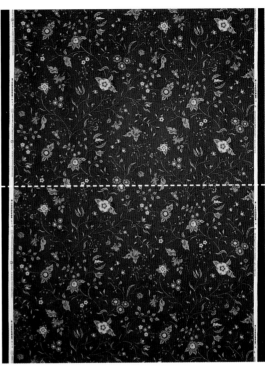

For tightly woven patterned decorator fabric, mark both selvages at the exact same point in the pattern repeat. Using a long straightedge, draw a line connecting the two points. If you will be stitching two or more full widths of fabric together, make all the cuts at the same location in the repeat. This usually means that you cut the pieces longer than necessary, stitch them together, and then trim them to the necessary length.

QUICK REFERENCE

Printed on-grain. This means the pattern repeat coincides exactly with the crosswise grain of the fabric. To test fabric before you buy, place it on a flat surface and fold the cut edge back, aligning the selvages on the sides. Crease the fold with your fingers, then unfold the fabric and check to see if the crease runs into the selvage at exactly the same point in the pattern on both sides. Slight differences of less than 2" (5 cm) can usually be corrected by stretching the fabric diagonally. Avoid buying fabric that is printed more that 2" (5 cm) off-grain, as you will not be able to correct it, and the finished project will not hang straight.

Matching Designs

Stitching seams in decorator fabrics that have printed designs or woven-in patterns requires a few extra steps to make sure the pattern will flow uninterrupted from one fabric width to the next.

How to Match a Design

1 Place two fabric widths right sides together, aligning the selvages. Fold back the upper selvage until the pattern matches. Adjust the top layer slightly up or down so that the pattern lines up exactly. Press the foldline.

2 Unfold the pressed selvage, and pin the fabric widths together, inserting the pins in and parallel to the foldline.

3 Turn the fabric over, and check the match from the right side. Make any necessary adjustments.

4 Repin the fabric so the pins are perpendicular to the foldline. Stitch the seam following the foldline; remove the pins as you come to them.

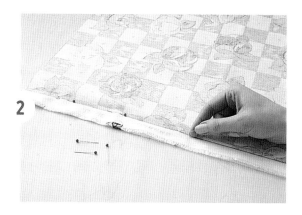

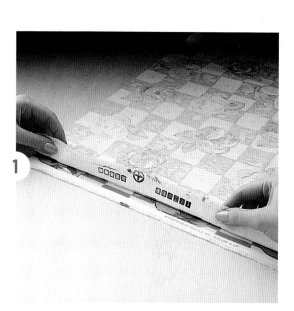

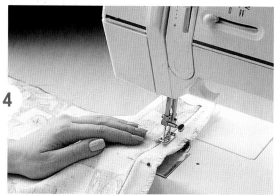

5 Check the match from the right side again. Make any necessary adjustments. Trim away the selvages, cutting the seam allowances to ½" (1.3 cm).

6 Set the pattern selector to *zigzag* and your stitch width and length to medium. *Finish the raw edges together* by zigzagging down the length of the seam. Press the seam allowances to one side.

7 Trim the entire fabric panel to the necessary cut length as determined in the project instructions. (Remember your initial cut length for the patterned fabric included extra length to accommodate the pattern repeat.)

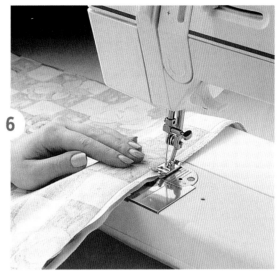

QUICK REFERENCE

Zigzag. The sewing machine needle moves from side to side with each stitch. You can adjust the width and length of the zigzag. Experiment with different settings on a scrap of fabric.

Finish the raw edges together. This prevents the fabric from raveling, which is especially important for home décor items that are not lined.

Selecting a Pattern

Major pattern companies follow a uniform sizing based on standard body measurements. This is not exactly the same as ready-to-wear sizing.

Determining Size

To select the right pattern size, first take your standard body measurements. Wear your usual undergarments and use a tape measure that doesn't stretch. It may be easier to have another person measure you. Record your measurements and compare them with the size chart on the back of the pattern or in the back of the pattern book.

Taking Standard Body Measurements

1 Waistline. Tie a string or piece of elastic around your middle, and allow it to roll to your natural waistline. Measure at this exact location with a tape measure. Leave the string in place as a reference for measuring your hips and back waist length.

2 Hips. Measure around the fullest part of your hips. This is usually 7" to 9" (18 to 23 cm) below the waistline, depending on your height.

3 Bust. Place the tape measure under your arms, across the widest part of the back and the fullest part of the bustline.

4 Back waist length. Measure from the middle of the most prominent bone at the base of the neck down to the waistline string.

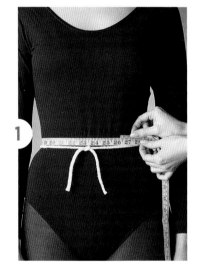

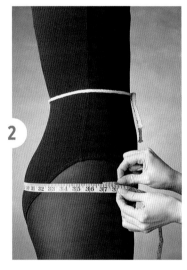

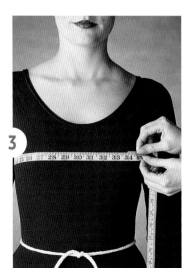

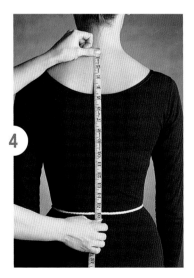

Pattern Selection

Selecting a pattern for a garment allows for more creativity than shopping from a ready-to-wear catalog. Pattern catalogs don't limit you to certain fabric, colors, skirt lengths, or types of trims shown on the pages. You are free to choose a combination of features that best reflect your style and are most flattering to you.

Major pattern companies publish new catalogs with each season, which means that designer trends seen in clothing stores are reflected in the newest pattern catalogs along with more classic styles. You'll find simple patterns for sewers who prefer the quick and easy styles, and more detailed patterns for experienced sewers. The number of pattern pieces listed on the back of the pattern will provide a clue to the complexity of the pattern. The fewer pieces, the easier the project. Also, the pattern may indicate whether it is intended for knits only.

Pattern catalogs are usually divided into categories by garment types and marked by index tabs. The newest fashions often appear in the first few pages of each category. Pattern illustrations are accompanied by information on recommended fabrics and yardage requirements. An index at the back of the catalog lists patterns in numerical order along with their page numbers. The back of the catalog also includes a complete size chart for every figure type..

All About Patterns

The pattern envelope is a selling tool and an educational device. The front generally has a photograph of the finished garment and several drawings of the variations that can be sewn using the pattern. On the pattern back, you'll find detailed information to help you select fabric and all the notions necessary to complete your project.

The Envelope Front

Pattern company name, and style number that corresponds to the number in the catalog, are displayed prominently.

Size or sizes included in the pattern are indicated near the number. Most patterns include several sizes.

Photograph or fashion illustration shows the main pattern design made up in suitable fabrics. It also indicates how closely or loosely the pattern is intended to fit.

Labels may indicate special considerations: that a pattern is suitable for knits only, is easy to sew, has special fitting or size-related information.

Views, labeled with letters, are alternate designs that can be sewn using the pattern. They may include variations in length, fullness, or other design details.

The Envelope Back

Fabric amounts required for each view in all the available sizes are listed in a chart. Locate the style view and the fabric width at the left; match it with your size at the top. The number where the two columns meet is the amount of fabric you need to buy. Interfacing (page 32) and elastic (page 32) requirements are also listed. Metric equivalents are given in a separate chart.

Fabrics recommended for sewing the garments are listed to help you make your selections. This paragraph will also tell you if certain fabrics are unsuitable, such as stripes or one-way designs.

Style number is repeated on the pattern back.

Number of pattern pieces gives you an idea of how easy or complicated the pattern is to sew.

Descriptions of the garment include its style, how it is intended to fit, and construction information for each of the views.

Notions, such as thread, buttons, and zippers, are listed in another paragraph.

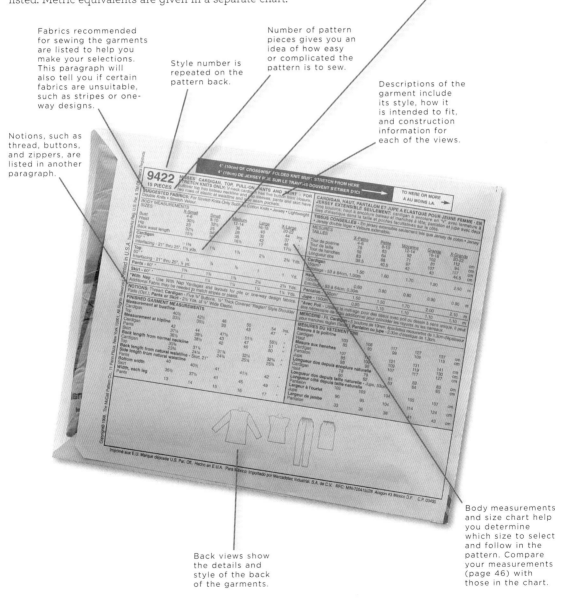

Back views show the details and style of the back of the garments.

Body measurements and size chart help you determine which size to select and follow in the pattern. Compare your measurements (page 46) with those in the chart.

Inside the Pattern

Even if you love a good puzzle, your first peek at the pattern innards can be scary. Here's what to expect.

Pattern Features

Detailed sketches show you both front and back of each view.

General sewing directions, given as a short refresher course, include a key to the symbols used on the pattern pieces, and some basic construction techniques.

Cutting layouts for different fabric widths are shown for each view, in every size. Alternative layouts are shown for fabric with or without nap.

Pattern key, identifying every pattern piece by name and number.

Sewing directions are a step-by-step guide through the construction of the garment. Each step is accompanied by a sketch. The right side of the fabric usually appears shaded; the wrong side is plain. Interfacing is often indicated with dots.

Pattern Layout

All pattern companies use a universal system of symbols on their pattern pieces. These symbols help you lay out the pattern, show you where to cut, help you match up seamlines, show you where to sew, and give placement guides for things like buttons, buttonholes, and hems. Along with the symbols, you will also find essential instructions printed on the pattern pieces.

Foldline. Often indicated by a long bracket with arrows at each end, it may have "place on fold" instructions. Place the pattern piece with the foldline exactly on the fold of the fabric.

Dots (large and small), squares, or triangles found along the seamlines indicate areas of construction where precise matching, clipping, or stitching is essential.

Grainline. Heavy solid line with arrows at each end. Place the pattern piece on the fabric with the grainline running parallel to the selvage.

Adjustment line. Double line indicating where the pattern can be lengthened or shortened before cutting out the fabric. If an alteration is necessary, cut the pattern on the double line; spread evenly to lengthen, or overlap evenly to shorten.

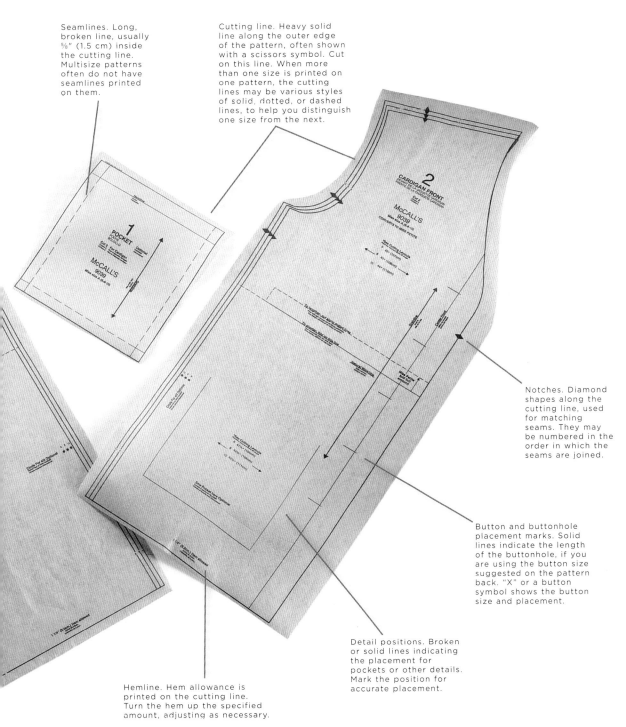

Seamlines. Long, broken line, usually ⅝" (1.5 cm) inside the cutting line. Multisize patterns often do not have seamlines printed on them.

Cutting line. Heavy solid line along the outer edge of the pattern, often shown with a scissors symbol. Cut on this line. When more than one size is printed on one pattern, the cutting lines may be various styles of solid, dotted, or dashed lines, to help you distinguish one size from the next.

Notches. Diamond shapes along the cutting line, used for matching seams. They may be numbered in the order in which the seams are joined.

Button and buttonhole placement marks. Solid lines indicate the length of the buttonhole, if you are using the button size suggested on the pattern back. "X" or a button symbol shows the button size and placement.

Detail positions. Broken or solid lines indicating the placement for pockets or other details. Mark the position for accurate placement.

Hemline. Hem allowance is printed on the cutting line. Turn the hem up the specified amount, adjusting as necessary.

Pattern Layout continued

Prepare a large work area, such as a dining room table covered with a cutting board (page 32). Assemble all the pattern pieces you will be needing, and press out any wrinkles with a warm, dry iron.

Locate and circle the correct pattern layout diagram (page 51) on your pattern guide sheet. These diagrams usually show you the easiest, most efficient way to lay out your pattern. Some fabrics have a nap, meaning they have definite up and down directions. For these fabrics, pattern pieces must all be laid out in the same direction.

Fold the fabric in half, lengthwise. Smooth it out on the work surface, so that the selvages align and the crosswise grain is perpendicular to them. Arrange the pattern pieces as indicated in the layout diagram. White pattern shapes indicate the piece is to be placed with the printed side up. Shaded pieces are to be placed with the printed side down. Be sure to follow any other incidental directions that pertain to your layout. After all the pieces are in place, pin them to the fabric. Do not begin cutting until all the pattern pieces are in place.

Pinning

1 First, position the pattern pieces that are to be cut on the fold. Place each one directly on the folded edge of the fabric. Pin the corners diagonally. Then continue pinning near the outer edge, placing the pins parallel to the cutting line. Space the pins about 3" (7.5 cm) apart; closer together on curves.

2 Place the straight-grain pattern pieces on the fabric, with the grainline arrow parallel to the selvages on woven fabrics or parallel to the ribs on knits. Measure from each end of the arrow to the selvage, shifting the pattern until the distances are equal. Pin both ends of the grainline so the pattern will not shift. Then pin the outer edges.

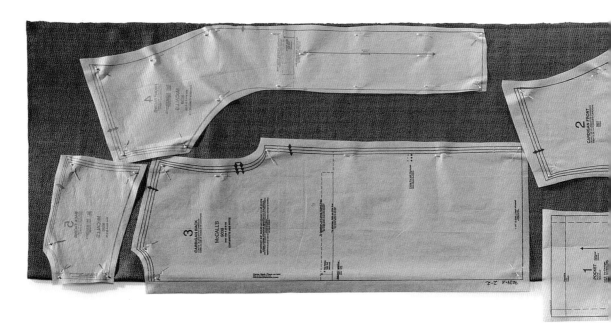

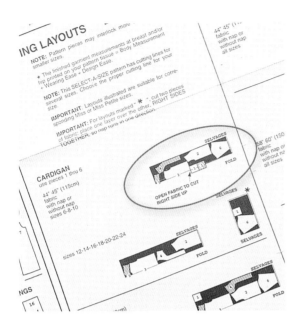

QUICK REFERENCE

Fold the fabric in half, lengthwise. When your fabric is folded like this, you will end up with mirror-image pieces for the left and right sides of the garment. Pattern directions usually suggest folding right sides together. Sometimes there are advantages to folding wrong sides together, such as having a better view of the fabric design or ease in marking. Either way will work.

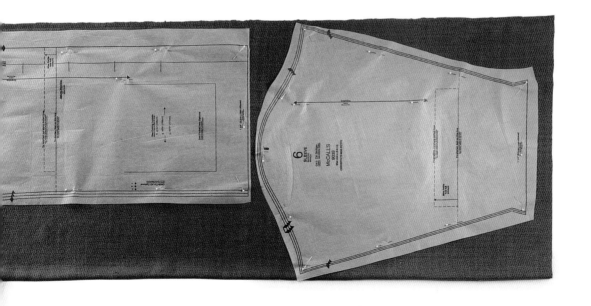

Cutting and Marking

Don't be intimidated! Locate the correct cutting lines, and cut with confidence. Transfer the necessary marks, and you'll be ready to sew!

Cutting

Accuracy is important, since mistakes made in cutting cannot always be corrected. Before cutting, double-check the placement of the pattern pieces.

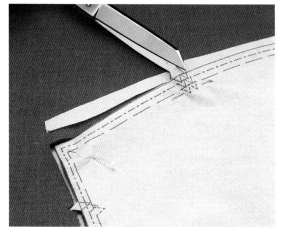

Using bent-handled shears, cut with long, firm strokes, cutting directly on the cutting line. Take shorter strokes around curves. If you are using a multisize pattern, be sure that you follow the correct cutting line all the time.

Notches can be cut outward, especially if the fabric is loosely woven or if the pattern calls for ¼" (6 mm) seam allowances. Cut multiple notches as one unit, not separately. Or, you can cut directly through the notches, and then mark them with short snips into the seam allowances.

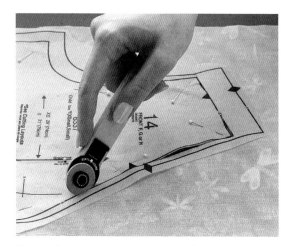

If you prefer to use a rotary cutter and mat, be sure to keep the mat under the area being cut. Use steady, even pressure, and, above all, keep fingers and small children away from the rotary cutter.

Marking

Keep the pattern pieces pinned in place after cutting. Transfer pattern symbols to the appropriate side of the fabric, using one of the following methods.

Pins are a quick way to transfer marks. Since they may fall out easily, use pin marks only when you intend to sew immediately. Or, pin-mark first, remove the pattern, and mark again, using chalk or erasable fabric marker.

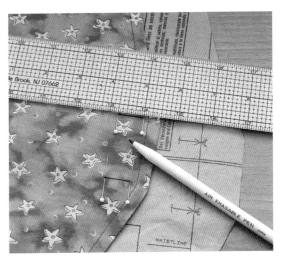

Erasable fabric markers are felt-tip pens designed specifically for sewing needs. Air-erasable marks disappear within 48 hours. Water-erasable marks disappear with a spritz of water.

Chalk is available in pencil form or as a powder in a rolling-wheel dispenser.

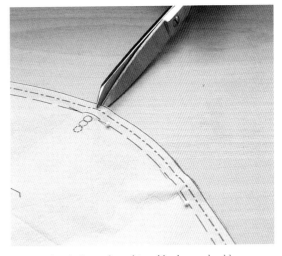

Snips are handy for marking things like dots at shoulder seams. Make shallow snips into the seam allowances at the dot locations.

Sewing Garments

The six projects in this section are basic wardrobe pieces. In each project, you will learn a few new sewing skills. If you work your way through the projects in order, your skill set will be fairly complete by the time you finish your first unlined jacket. As you repeat techniques you've learned in previous projects, your confidence will grow.

Five of the six projects require a commercial pattern, so look for a pattern that closely resembles the lines and detail level of the garment shown. Certainly you should read the pattern instructions, but use the book instructions and photographs to sew your garment. You do not need a commercial pattern to sew the apron.

T-Shirts

T-shirts are classic and versatile; it seems you can never have too many. As you become more experienced, you'll be surprised how quickly you are able to make them. The fun begins in selecting your knit fabric (page 39) from the array of stripes, prints, and colorful solids available. To help you decide which pattern to buy, note the way the T-shirts fit the models or sketches on the pattern envelope front. Some patterns are designed for an "oversized" look, others are meant to fit the form of your body more closely. Your pattern should have four pieces: front, back, sleeve, and neck ribbing. Some may also have a piece for sleeve ribbing.

The fit of the T-shirt will vary with the fabric's degree of stretch. T-shirt patterns, designed for knits only, indicate the amount of stretch required of the fabric. For instance, "25% stretch crosswise" would indicate that 4" (10 cm) of fabric will stretch on the crosswise grain an additional 1" (2.5 cm). Always test the degree of stretch in the fabric, especially if you are making a close-fitting T-shirt.

WHAT YOU'LL LEARN..

- Techniques for sewing with knits
- How to sew in sleeves
- How to apply ribbing to a neckline

WHAT YOU'LL NEED..

- T-shirt pattern (designed for stretch knits)
- Knit fabric (check pattern for amount)
- Scraps of fusible knit interfacing (page 32)
- Ribbing (check pattern for amount)
- Matching all-purpose thread

How to Sew a T-shirt

1 Prepare the fabric (page 41); however, don't wash the ribbing, as the raw edges are likely to stretch out of shape. T-shirts are easiest to sew using ¼" *(6 mm) seam allowances*. If your pattern pieces have ⅝" (1.5 cm) seam allowances, trim them down to ¼" (6 mm) before laying out the pattern. Lay out the pattern (page 52), and cut the fabric (page 56). Transfer any necessary marks (page 57). Insert a ballpoint sewing machine needle; size 11/70 or 12/80 is suitable for most knits. Cut two ½" (1.3 cm) strips of fusible interfacing the length of the shoulder seam. Place a strip even with the cut edge of each back shoulder, on the wrong side of the fabric. Fuse the strips in place, *following the manufacturer's directions*. This is done to *stabilize the shoulder seams*.

2 Place the T-shirt front over the back, right sides together, aligning the shoulder seam allowance edges. Pin, inserting the pins perpendicular to the edges. Stitch the front and back T-shirt sections together at the shoulder seams, using a ¼" (6 mm) seam allowance; *backstitch (p. 19)* a few stitches at each edge. Since the shoulder seams are stabilized, a straight stitch is appropriate here.

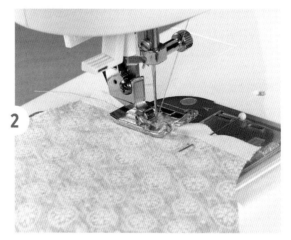

3 Add a second row of machine stitching (either a straight stitch or a narrow zigzag) next to the first row, within the seam allowance. Press the shoulder seam allowances toward the shirt back.

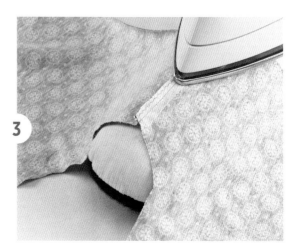

4 Mark the center front and center back of the neckline with pins. Then bring the two centers together and mark the points halfway between with pins. (These marks should be slightly ahead of the shoulder seams.) The neckline is now divided into fourths.

5 Sew the short ends of the **ribbing, right sides together**, forming a circle. Use ¼" (6 mm) seam allowance, and sew with a short straight stitch. **Press the seam open with your fingers**.

QUICK REFERENCE

¼" (6 mm) seam allowances. Some patterns made especially for knits are designed with ¼" (6 mm) seam allowances, rather than ⅝" (1.5 cm). In many cases, running the outside edge of the presser foot along the cut edge of the fabric results in a ¼" (6 mm) seam. Run a test to be sure.

Follow the manufacturer's directions. The interfacing bolt is wrapped with a long sheet of plastic on which the directions are printed. Have the store clerk cut off a section of the directions for you to take home.

Stabilize the shoulder seams. Shoulder seams follow the crosswise grain, the direction in which knit fabrics stretch the most. However, it is not desirable or necessary to have shoulder seams that stretch. Narrow strips of fusible interfacing help the seams keep their intended length. You'll also find that this makes sewing in the stretchy direction much easier.

Ribbing, right sides together. Sometimes knit fabrics and ribbings do not have a right or wrong side. To test, gently stretch the raw edge on the crosswise grain of the ribbing. If the edge curls to one side, that side is the right side of the fabric. If it doesn't curl to either side, either side can be used on the outside.

Press the seam open with your fingers. Avoid pressing ribbing with an iron, as this may destroy its elasticity.

6 Fold the ribbing in half, lengthwise, with the raw edges even and the seam allowances on the inside. Divide the ribbing into fourths, as you did the neckline. Mark these sections with pins.

(continued)

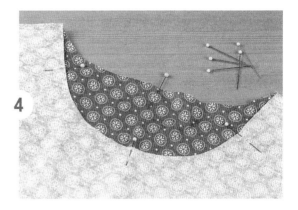

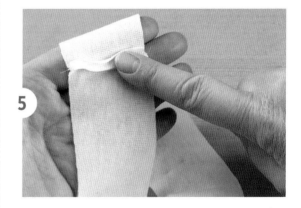

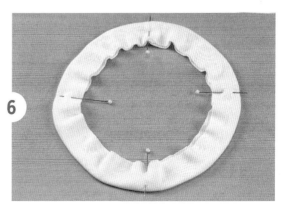

How to Sew a T-shirt continued

7 Pin the ribbing to the right side of the neck-line, aligning the ribbing seam to the center back pin mark; match up the remaining pin marks.

8 Place the fabric under the presser foot, with the ribbing facing up. Stitch with a narrow zigzag or stretch stitch (page 20), keeping the raw edges even and stretching the ribbing evenly to fit each section between pins. Remove the pins as you come to them.

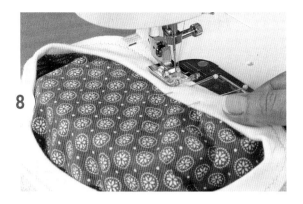

8

9 Stitch again next to the first row, using a narrow, medium-length zigzag stitch. Gently press the ribbing toward the shirt, being careful not to stretch the ribbing.

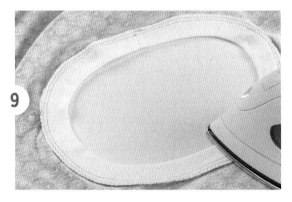

9

10 Make sure you have marked the top of the sleeve and any other notches on the sleeve and shirt as indicated on the pattern pieces. With right sides together, pin the sleeve to the armhole of the shirt, matching the top dot or notch to the shoulder seam, and aligning any other notches. Pin frequently, easing in any extra sleeve fullness.

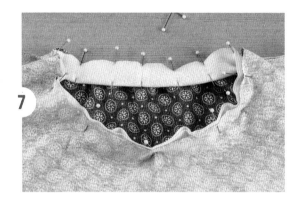

7

10

QUICK REFERENCE

Hem allowance. The pattern has allowed a predetermined extra length for turning under and finishing the sleeves and lower edge. This amount is indicated on your pattern.

11 Stitch the armhole seam, using a narrow, medium-length zigzag stitch; remove the pins as you come to them. Stitch again next to the first row, within the seam allowance.

12 Repeat steps 10 and 11 for the other sleeve. Press the seams toward the sleeves. With the right sides together, pin the shirt front to the shirt back along the sides and sleeves, matching the underarm seams.

13 Stitch and finish the seams in the same manner as for the sleeve seams, beginning at the lower edge of the shirt and sewing continuously to the lower edge of the sleeve. Press the seams toward the back.

14 Turn under the lower *hem allowance*, as specified by your pattern. Stitch the hem by hand (page 24) or by machine (page 25); select a method that will allow the hem to stretch, if necessary. Hem the lower edges of the sleeves in the same manner.

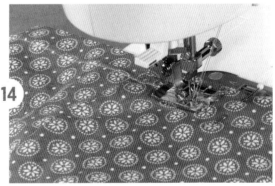

TIP You can press the side seams, simply by slipping the shirt over the end of the ironing board. Insert a seam roll or sleeve board (page 31) into the sleeve, so you can press the seam allowance to the side without pressing unwanted creases into the opposite side of the sleeve.

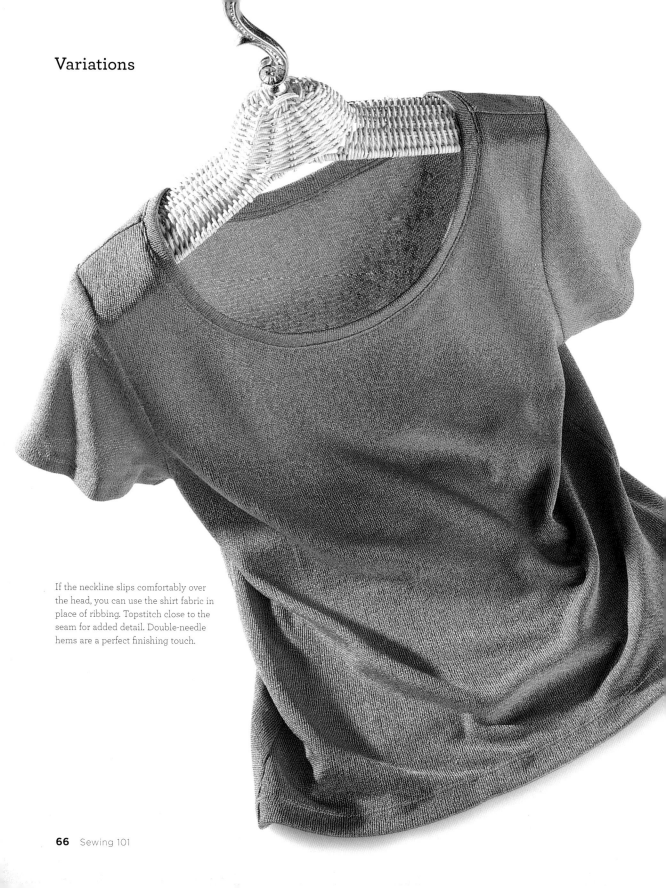

Variations

If the neckline slips comfortably over the head, you can use the shirt fabric in place of ribbing. Topstitch close to the seam for added detail. Double-needle hems are a perfect finishing touch.

Kids love T-shirts. The sleeves can be finished with ribbing by following the directions for the neckline ribbing.

Mock turtleneck or turtleneck styles are created with wider ribbing pieces. Ribbing fabric is often dyed to match other knits.

Pull-on Skirts

Skirts with elastic waistbands are classic, comfortable, and easy-care. Straight or flared versions in varying lengths can be coordinated with a variety of sweaters or other tops for business, dress, or casual wear. Check the pattern envelope for recommended fabrics. Some patterns are designed only for knits and generally fit the body closer, counting on the stretchiness of the fabric to allow you to slide the skirt over your hips. Patterns suitable for woven fabrics will include extra fullness. The first set of directions works for woven or knit fabrics. Alternate steps for sewing with knits begin on page 75. These directions may differ from your pattern; be sure to use the seam allowance given in your pattern. Select a pattern with two pieces: a front and a back. An elastic casing at the waistline is formed from excess fabric length at the skirt top. The skirt itself may be constructed of two, three, or four sections, depending on whether or not there are center front or back seams.

WHAT YOU'LL LEARN . . . .

- Two methods for sewing elastic waistlines
- Hem alternatives for skirts
- How to sew and finish side, front, and back seams

WHAT YOU'LL NEED . . . .

- Skirt pattern with elastic waistline
- Fabric (check pattern for amount)
- Matching all-purpose thread
- 1" (2.5 cm) nonroll elastic, enough to go around your waist

How to Sew a Pull-on Skirt

1 To construct the skirt following these directions, 2¾" (7 cm) of fabric must be allowed for the casing above the waistline. This may be different from the casing allowance already on your pattern. Measure this distance from the waistline, and mark a cutting line on your pattern. (Add extra paper, if necessary.) Be sure to mark both front and back pattern pieces.

(continued)

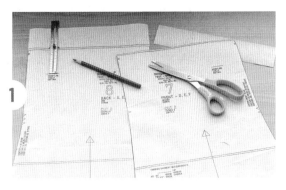

How to Sew a Pull-on Skirt *continued*

2 Prepare the fabric (page 41), lay out the pattern (page 52), and cut the fabric (page 56). Transfer any necessary marks (page 57). Insert a size 11/70 or 12/80 sharp or universal sewing machine needle. If your pattern does not have center front or back seams, move on to step 4. If your pattern has a center front seam, place the skirt front pieces right sides together, aligning the center cut edges and matching the notches. Insert pins perpendicular to the center front seam.

3 Place the fabric under the presser foot with the cut edges aligned to the ⅝" (1.5 cm) seam allowance guide. Stitch the center front seam, **backstitching (p. 17)** a few stitches at the upper and lower edges. If your pattern has a center back seam, stitch it in the same manner.

 TIP If your skirt has side seam pockets, follow the pattern directions carefully because methods vary greatly.

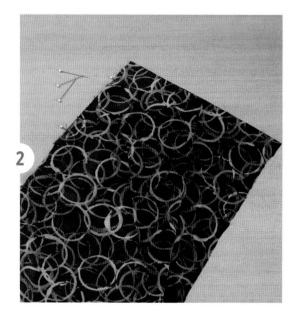

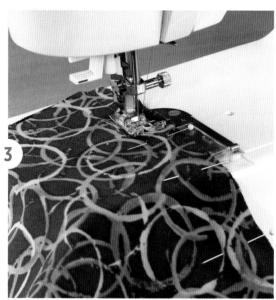

TIP Be sure you are not pinning the pieces together along the side seams. Sometimes it is difficult to tell the difference. Check your pattern to be sure.

4 Place the front and back skirt pieces right sides together, aligning the side edges and matching the notches. ***Insert pins perpendicular to the sides (p. 19)***. Stitch the side seams, backstitching at the upper and lower edges, and ***removing pins as you come to them (p. 19)***. If you are sewing on a woven fabric, finish (page 21) the edges of all the seam allowances.

5 Press all the seams flat to set the stitching line in the fabric. This may seem unnecessary, but it really does give you a better-looking seam in the end. Then press the seam allowances open.

TIP To prevent the cut edge of the seam allowance from imprinting the front of the fabric, press seams open over a seam roll or hard cardboard tube.

(continued)

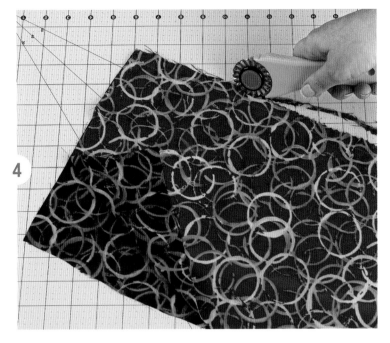

4

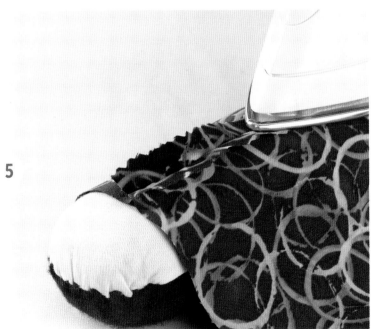

5

How to Sew a Pull-on Skirt continued

6 Baste the seam allowances open flat from the upper edge down about 4" (10 cm) (arrow). This will keep them from getting in the way when you insert the elastic in step 9. Finish the waistline edge, using a multistitch-zigzag (page 21). Fold the upper edge 1½" (3.8 cm) to the wrong side, and press. Insert pins along and perpendicular to the fold.

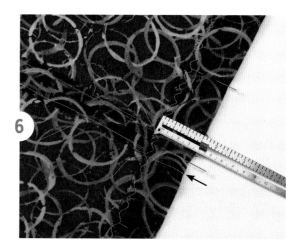

7 Edgestitch close to the fold around the upper edge of the waistline. Begin and end at a side seam, overlapping the stitches about ½" (1.3 cm).

TIP Sometimes it is difficult to tell the skirt front from the back when the garment is finished. We've sewn a short loop of twill tape under the casing seam to identify the back.

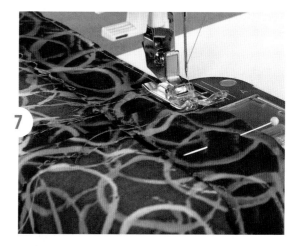

8 Insert pins along the lower edge of the casing. Place a piece of tape on the bed of your machine 1¼" (3.2 cm) from the tip of the needle. Stitch the lower edge of the casing, guiding the upper edge along the tape. Leave a 2" (5 cm) opening at one side seam.

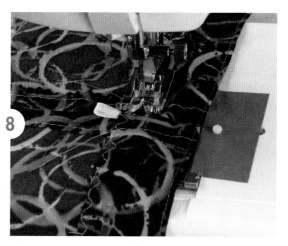

9 Fasten a safety pin or bodkin (page 32) to one end of the elastic, and insert the elastic through the casing opening. Push and pull the safety pin all the way to the opposite side of the opening. Remove the basting threads from step 6.

TIP Insert a large safety pin across the free end of the elastic so that it will not get pulled into the opening.

10 Try on the skirt. Pull up the elastic to fit your waist snugly, yet comfortably; pin the ends together. Take off the skirt, and trim the overlapped ends to ½" (1.3 cm), if necessary.

11 Pull the pinned ends of the elastic several inches (centimeters) out of the casing. Place them under the presser foot, and stitch through both layers, using a multistitch-zigzag. To reinforce, stitch again.

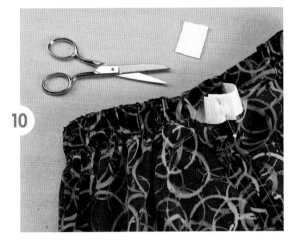

(continued)

How to Sew a Pull-on Skirt *continued*

12 Machine-stitch the opening in the casing closed. Distribute the casing fullness evenly around the elastic. **Stitch in the ditch** at the seams (arrow) to keep the elastic from shifting or rolling.

13 Try on the skirt, and have someone **mark the hem length** for you, using chalk or pins. Take off the skirt, and trim the hem allowance to an even depth. (Check the pattern for hem allowance.) Turn under the hem along the markings, and pin. Press. For double-fold hems on slightly flared skirts, it is helpful to hand-baste on the inner fold.

14 Stitch the hem by hand (page 24) or by machine (page 25); select a method that will allow the hem to stretch, if you are using a knit. Give the skirt a final pressing, and give yourself a pat on the back.

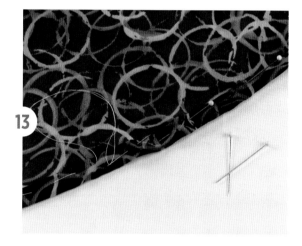

QUICK REFERENCE

Stitch in the ditch. Stitching from the right side and using short stitches, stitch directly into the well of the seam. Your stitches will practically disappear.

Mark the hem length. During the marking, stand straight, wearing the shoes you will be wearing with the skirt. The person marking should measure up from the floor to the desired length, moving around you as necessary. Otherwise, the hem will be uneven. If you don't have help, turn up the hem to the desired length all the way around and check in a mirror for even length.

Twice the width of the elastic. For this method, 1" (2.5 cm) elastic works well, though you may decide to use a different width. Some specialty elastics have channels for topstitching, giving the look of multiple rows.

Alternate Steps for a Knit Pull-on Skirt

1 To construct a knit skirt following these directions, an amount of fabric equal to **twice the
width of the elastic** must be allowed above the
waistline. Measure this distance from the waistline,
and mark a new cutting line on your pattern.
(Add extra paper, if necessary.) Be sure to mark
both front and back pattern pieces. Follow steps
2 to 5 on pages 70 and 71, sewing with the seam
allowances designated by your pattern. It is not
necessary to finish seams on knit skirts.

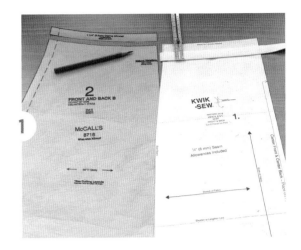

TIP Read your pattern directions. Some patterns,
especially those that have ¼" (6 mm) seam allowances, instruct you to sew your elastic waistline
with this method. There is no need to alter those patterns, as
they already allow this amount of fabric at the top.

2 Cut a piece of elastic to fit your waist snugly,
yet still stretch to fit over your hips. Overlap
the ends ½" (1.3 cm), and stitch them together,
using a wide zigzag stitch or multistitch-zigzag.
Divide both the elastic and the upper edge of the
skirt into fourths, and pin-mark. Pin the elastic to
the wrong side of the skirt, aligning the edges and
matching the pin marks; insert the pins perpendicular to the edges.

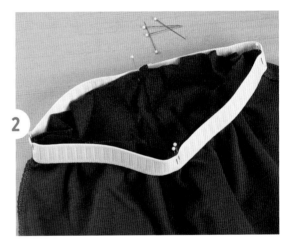

(continued)

Alternate Steps for a Knit Pull-on Skirt continued

3 Insert four more pins, evenly spaced, between the quarter marks, distributing the fabric fullness evenly. Set your machine for a medium-width multistitch-zigzag. Place the skirt under the presser foot with the elastic on top. Align the edge of the foot to the elastic and fabric edges. Stitch, **stretching the elastic to fit between the pins** and keeping the edges aligned. Remove pins as you come to them, stopping with the needle down in the fabric.

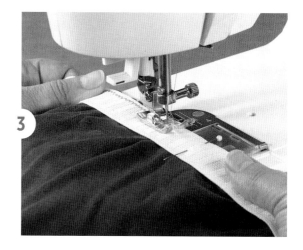

4 Fold the elastic to the wrong side of the skirt, so the fabric encases the elastic. From the right side of the skirt, **stitch in the ditch (p. 74)** of the seam through all the waistband layers, at each seam. This step makes step 5 easier.

TIP Stretch the waistband slightly to give yourself a clear view of your target.

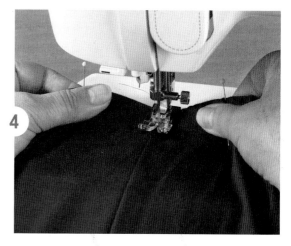

5 With the right side facing up, topstitch through all layers of the waistband, stretching the elastic as you sew. Use either a zigzag or multistitch-zigzag, with medium width and length, and stitch near the lower edge of the elastic. These stitches will allow the skirt to stretch as it goes over your hips. Finish the skirt, following steps 13 and 14 on page 74.

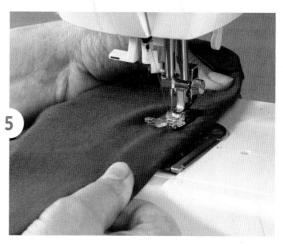

QUICK REFERENCE

Stretching the elastic to fit between the pins. Grasp the fabric and elastic behind the presser foot with one hand and ahead of the presser foot with the other hand, working in small sections at a time. Stretch the elastic only far enough to take up the slack in the fabric. Keep an even tension on the elastic, allowing the feed dogs to feed the fabric at a steady pace. Stop sewing to move your hands.

Simple Skirt Variations

For woven skirts, sew multiple-channel casings to handle two rows of ⅜" (1 cm) elastic or three rows of ¼" (6 mm) elastic. See the directions for pull-on pants (page 79). To create this look with knit fabric, sew in one circle of wide elastic that has channels for topstitching (page 32).

Vary the hem treatment (pages 24 and 25) to suit the skirt style or to add design interest. A narrow, double-fold hem is suitable for a slightly flared skirt. Use a double-needle hem to give knits a little stretch. Stitch invisible hems in dressy skirts, either by hand or by machine.

Pull-on Pants

Pull-on pants with elastic waists are easy to fit and easy to sew. When sewn in supple, lightweight wovens, such as rayon or microfiber, they are elegant enough for evening wear. For sportier looks, cotton, cotton blends, linen, or seersucker work well and can be paired with simple T-shirts or blouses. Consider purchasing enough fabric to make a matching jacket or vest to go with your pants and complete the outfit.

Select a pants pattern with two main pieces: the front and the back. The elastic casing for the waist is formed from excess fabric at the top. These instructions are for pants without pockets. The method for sewing side-seam pockets varies from pattern to pattern. Once you understand the basics of sewing pull-on pants, you can advance to a pattern with pockets, following the pattern instructions closely.

WHAT YOU'LL LEARN...............

- How to alter the crotch length of a pattern
- How to alter the leg length of a pattern
- How to make a multi-row elastic waistband

WHAT YOU'LL NEED...............

- Pants pattern; loose-fitting with elastic waistline
- Fabric (check pattern for amount)
- Matching all-purpose thread
- ⅜" (1 cm) elastic, enough to go twice around your waist

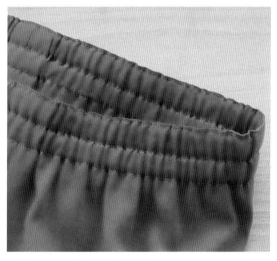

The waistband casing on these pants is divided in half with a stitching line to accommodate two elastic strips.

How to Sew Pull-on Pants

1 Measure the length of the crotch seam on a
pair of pants that you know fits comfortably.
Start from the bottom of the waistband in the front
and measure the distance around the crotch to
the bottom of the waistband in the back. On your
pattern, measure the total crotch length, standing
the tape measure on edge and measuring along the
seamline of the center front and center back. Begin
and end at the waistline mark; don't include the ⅝"
(1.5 cm) seam allowances at the inseam.

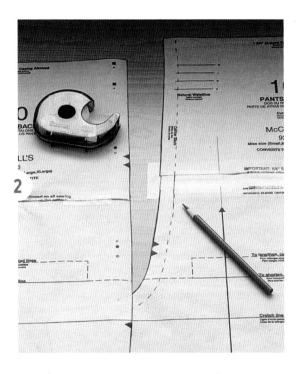

2 Compare the pants crotch length to the
pattern crotch length. Alter your pattern,
if necessary. Cut the pattern pieces apart on the
horizontal adjustment line. Then lap the pieces **by
half the total amount needed** to shorten (left),
or separate the pieces by half the total amount
needed to lengthen (right). Insert a paper strip to
lengthen; tape the pieces in place.

3 Next, compare the inseam measurements on
your pants and on your pattern, measuring
from the crotch seamline to the hemline. Make
any necessary alteration at the horizontal adjustment line.

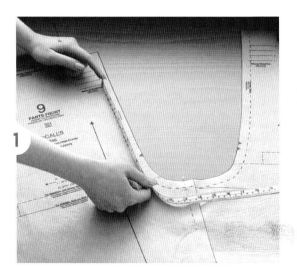

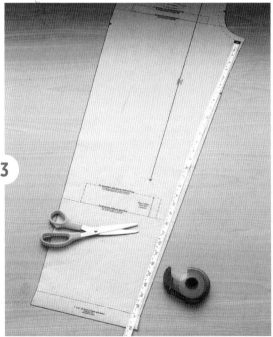

4 To construct the pants following these directions, 2¾" (7 cm) of fabric must be allowed for the casing above the waistline. Measure this distance from the waistline, and mark a new cutting line on your pattern. (Add extra paper, if necessary.) Be sure to mark both front and back pattern pieces.

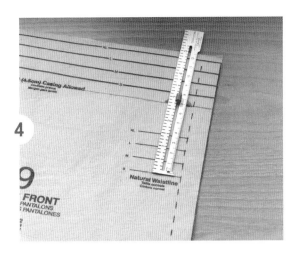

5 Prepare the fabric (page 41), lay out the pattern (page 52), and cut the fabric (page 56). Transfer any necessary marks (page 57). Set your sewing machine on a straight stitch of 10 to 12 stitches per inch, which is 2 to 2.5 mm. Insert a sewing machine needle suitable for your fabric (page 10). Place the right front over the right back, right sides together, along the inner leg. Pin them together, matching notches and *inserting the pins perpendicular to the edges (p.19)*. Stitch the seam, using ⅝" (1.5 cm) seam allowance unless your pattern indicates another seam allowance. Repeat for the left front and back legs.

6 Finish the edges of the seam allowances (page 21). Press the seams flat; then press them open.

(continued)

QUICK REFERENCE

By half the total amount needed. For example, if you need to shorten the crotch 1" (2.5 cm), shorten the pants front ½" (1.3 cm), and shorten the pants back ½" (1.3 cm).

How to Sew Pull-on Pants continued

7 With right sides together, pin the sewn right and left pants sections together at the crotch seam. Line up the inner leg seams, and match any notches. Stitch the entire seam. Then stitch the curved area of the seam between the notches a second time, ¼" (6 mm) from the first stitching.

8 Trim the seam in the curved area of the crotch close to the second stitching line. Finish the trimmed seam allowances. Then also finish the remaining seam allowances separately. Press the seam allowances open in the front and back, above the trimmed portion of the seam.

9 Pin the front and back, right sides together, at the side seams, matching notches and any other marks. Stitch a ⅝" (1.5 cm) seam from the bottom of the leg to the upper edge. Repeat for the other side seam.

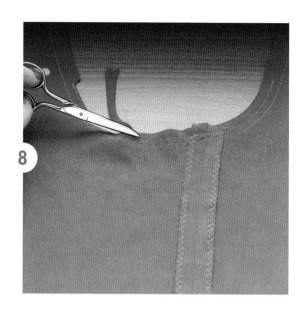

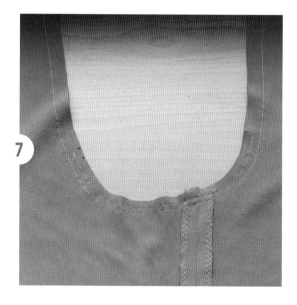

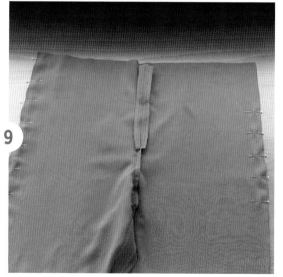

10 Finish the seam allowances separately. Press the seams flat; then press them open, using a seam roll. Baste all the seam allowances open flat from the upper edge down about 4" (10 cm). This will keep them from getting in the way when you insert the elastic in step 15.

11 Finish the waistline (page 21). Fold the upper edge 1½" (3.8 cm) to the wrong side, and press. Insert pins along and perpendicular to the fold.

12 Edgestitch close to the fold around the upper edge of the waistline. Begin and end at a side seam, overlapping the stitches about ½" (1.3 cm).

(continued)

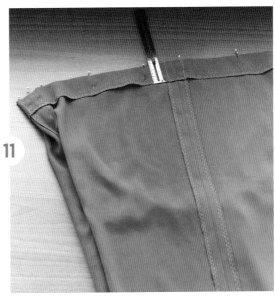

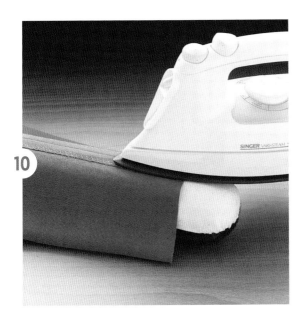

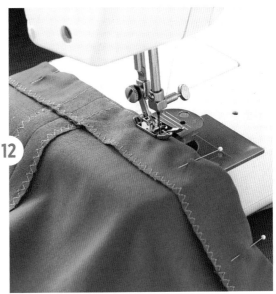

13 Place a piece of tape on the bed of your machine 1¼" (3.2 cm) from the tip of the needle. Stitch the lower edge of the casing, guiding the upper edge along the tape. Leave a 2" (5 cm) opening at one side seam.

14 Measure from the upper edge of the waist to a point halfway between the two stitching lines. Place tape on the machine bed as a sewing guide. Stitch, leaving a 2" (5 cm) opening just above the first opening.

TIP To use three rows of ¼" (6 mm) elastic in your waistline casing, divide the space into even thirds.

15 Cut two pieces of ⅜" (1 cm) elastic a little larger than your waist measurement. Fasten a safety pin or bodkin (page 32) to one end of one elastic, and insert the elastic through the casing opening into the top channel. Push and pull the safety pin through all the way to the opposite side of the opening, taking care not to let the free end disappear into the opening. Then do the same with the second piece of elastic, inserting it into the lower channel. Secure the ends of both pieces with safety pins.

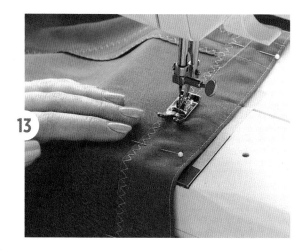

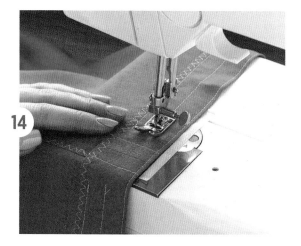

16 Try on the pants. Pull up the elastic to fit your waist snugly, yet comfortably; pin the ends together. Take off the pants. Pull the pinned ends of the top elastic several inches (centimeters) out of the casing. Trim the overlapped ends to ½" (1.3 cm), if necessary. Place them under the presser foot, and stitch through both layers, using a multis-titch zigzag. Repeat for the lower elastic.

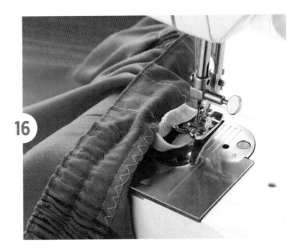

17 Machine-stitch the openings in the casing closed. Distribute the casing fullness evenly around the elastic. **Stitch in the ditch (p. 74)** at the seams to keep the elastic from shifting or rolling. Remove the basting stitches from step 10.

18 Turn under the hem allowance, and pin in place. Try on the pants, and adjust the length, if necessary. Take off the pants, and trim the hem allowance to an even depth. Press the fold. Finish the lower edge. Stitch the hem by hand (page 24) or by machine (page 25). Give the pants a final pressing, and they're ready to wear!

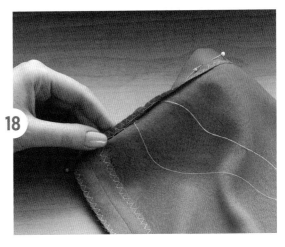

Vests

Vests, in a variety of styles, enhance wardrobes by complementing skirts, slacks, or dresses. They can be worn over knit tops, turtlenecks, or blouses, to fit the occasion.

For easy sewing, we've selected a loose-fitting, lined vest. Look for a pattern with two main pattern pieces: a front and a back. Good choices of fabric for a loose-fitting vest include cotton, cotton blends, rayon, linen, denim, wool crepe, wool gabardine, and corduroy. Select lining fabric made specifically for that purpose, or use lightweight cotton or blends.

WHAT YOU'LL LEARN . . . .

- How to sew lining in a vest
- How to sew buttonholes
- How to sew on buttons

WHAT YOU'LL NEED . . . .

- Vest pattern; lined, loose-fitting, with button closure
- Fabric for vest (check pattern for amount)
- Lining fabric (check pattern for amount)
- Matching all-purpose thread
- Lightweight to medium-weight fusible interfacing (page 33),enough to back entire vest front
- Buttons

How to Sew a Vest

1 Prepare the fabric (page 41). Lay out the pattern (page 56) and cut the fabric for the vest back pieces, reserving enough fabric for the fronts. Fuse interfacing to the wrong side of the vest front fabric, ***following the manufacturer's directions (p. 63)***. Lift and move the iron as needed to cover the entire piece. This will give support to buttons and buttonholes.

(continued)

How to Sew a Vest continued

2 Lay out the vest front pieces on the interfaced fabric; cut. Lay out and cut the lining pieces. Transfer any necessary marks (page 57). Set your sewing machine on a straight stitch of 10 to 12 stitches per inch, which equals 2 to 2.5 mm. For most fabrics, a universal machine needle size 12/80 will work fine.

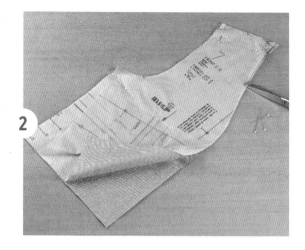

3 Place the vest fronts over the vest back, right sides together, aligning the shoulder seam allowance edges and matching any notches. **Insert pins** along the shoulders, **perpendicular to the cut edges (p. 19)**. Stitch ⅝" (1.5 cm) shoulder seams, **backstitching (p. 19)** at the beginning and end and **removing the pins as you come to them (p. 19)**.

4 Repeat step 3 for the lining pieces. For both the vest and the lining, press the shoulder seams flat; then press them open. **Press the lining side seam allowances under ⅝" (1.5 cm)**.

TIP Because all the seam allowances are going to be enclosed between the vest and the lining, it is not necessary to finish them.

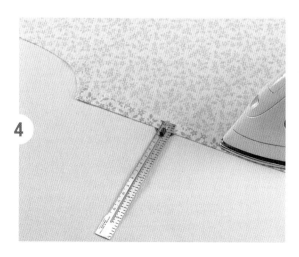

5 Place the vest and the lining right sides together, matching the raw edges and any notches. Insert pins perpendicular to the edges along all but the side seams.

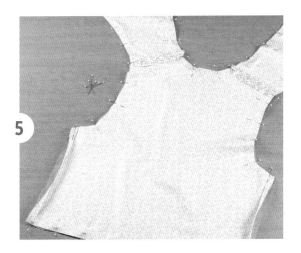

6 Stitch the ⅝" (1.5 cm) seam across the bottom of the vest back. Then stitch the armhole seams.

7 Beginning at the lower edge of one side, stitch one continuous seam along the bottom and center edges of one vest front, around the back neckline, and around the center and bottom edges of the other vest front, ending at the lower edge of the opposite side. Stop with the needle down in the fabric to pivot at each corner.

(continued)

> ## QUICK REFERENCE
> **Press the lining side seam allowances under ⅝"**
> **(1.5 cm).** You'll understand the importance of this when you get to steps 14 and 15. It is much easier to measure and press under the side seam allowances of the lining now, but unfold them to complete the next few steps.

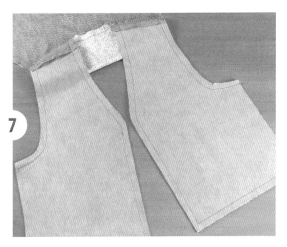

How to Sew a Vest continued

8 Trim the vest seam allowances to ¼" (6 mm); trim the lining seam allowances to ⅛" (3 mm). This step, called grading, reduces bulk. Do not trim the side seam allowances.

TIP Trimming to these widths works well for tightly woven fabrics. For looser weaves that tend to ravel easily, trim the seam allowances wider.

9 Clip into the curved neckline and armhole seam allowances every ½" (1.3 cm), clipping up to, but not through, the stitches. Clipping allows the seam allowance to turn smoothly to the inside and lie flat.

10 Put your hand through one of the open side seams of the back and through the shoulder of that side; grab the front of the vest. Pull it through the lining and vest at the shoulder and out the side seam, turning it right side out. Turn the other front right side out through the same side opening. Turn the back right side out.

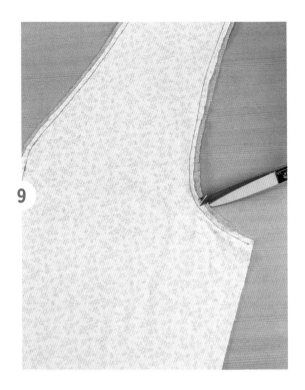

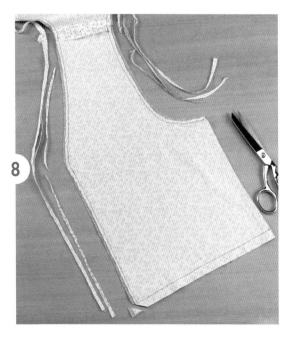

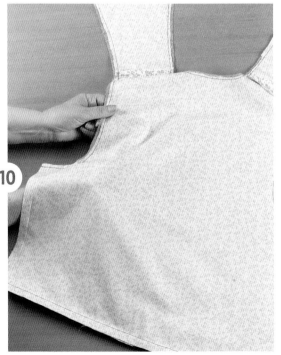

11 Insert a point turner (page 33) or similar tool into an opening, and gently push out any corners as necessary. Press all the seamed edges of the vest, centering the seam on the edge, with the lining to the inside.

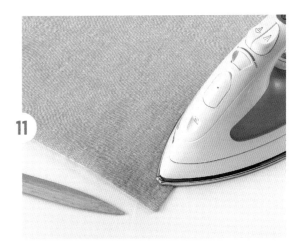

12 Pin the vest front and back, right sides together, along the side seams, keeping the lining free. Match up the armhole seams, placing a pin directly in the seamline and turning the seam allowances toward the lining. Match up the lower seams in the same way. Then pin the lining front and back together 1" to 2" (2.5 to 5 cm) beyond the seams.

13 Sew a ⅝" (1.5 cm) seam where you have pinned, **backstitching (p. 19)** at each end. As you cross the seam allowances at the armhole and lower edge, keep them turned toward the lining; remove pins as you come to them.

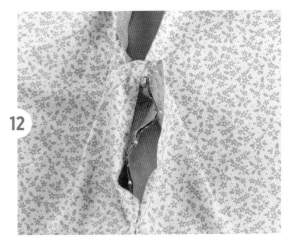

TIP This is an awkward seam to sew, especially at the beginning and end. Use the pressed foldlines of the lining (step 4) as seam guides there. Take your time, and be careful to keep the rest of the vest out of the way so that you do not catch unwanted fabric in the stitches.

(continued)

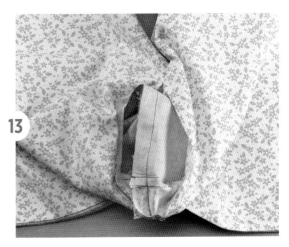

How to Sew a Vest continued

14 With your fingers, press the seam allowances open; turn in the lining seam allowances along the previously pressed lines. Press with your iron.

15 Pin the openings in the lining side seams closed. Slipstitch the edges together as on page 22.

16 Topstitch ⅜" (1 cm) from the edge, around the armholes and around the lower, front, and neck edges.

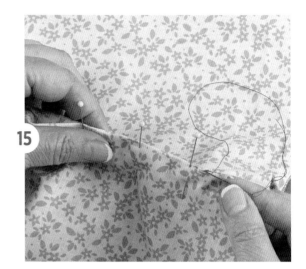

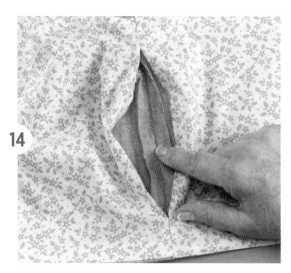

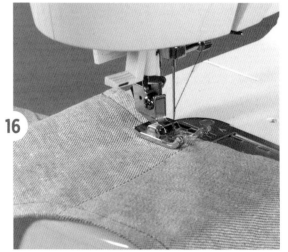

17 Transfer the buttonhole markings from your pattern to the vest (page 57). Make sure they are all the same distance from the front edge and uniform in size. Usually a buttonhole is ⅛" (3 mm) longer than the button diameter. To sew the buttonholes, follow the instructions in your sewing machine manual.

18 Overlap the vest fronts at the center front. Insert pins through the buttonholes at the outer ends; mark the locations for sewing the buttons on the other vest front.

19 Sew on the buttons as on page 23.

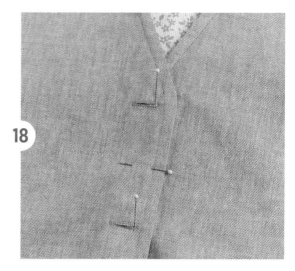

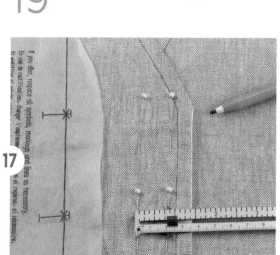

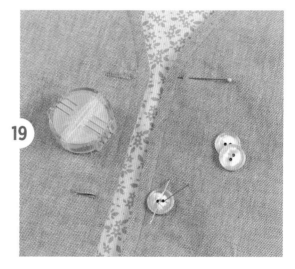

TIP Remember, buttonholes go on the right front for females or on the left front for males. Don't cut them open until you have double-checked for accuracy in placement and size.

TIP Running thread through beeswax before sewing on the buttons will make the thread stronger and help prevent it from tangling. After running the thread through beeswax, run it through your fingers to melt the wax into the thread.

Aprons

With the renewed interest in cooking and retro fashions, aprons have made a grand comeback. They can easily be made from a printed washable fabric. This style is made from six rectangles of fabric: a large rectangle for the skirt, two smaller rectangles for the pockets, two long narrow rectangles for ties, and one for the waistband. You don't need to buy a commercial pattern, you can simply measure and mark out the pieces on your fabric and cut them out. The skirt is gathered to a waistband with ties attached. Contrasting fabric was used for the pockets, waistband, and ties. Rickrack trim applied to the pockets and skirt hem give the apron a retro look.

WHAT YOU'LL LEARN.............

- How to gather fabric
- How to sew a waistband
- How to sew double-fold hems
- How to sew a patch pocket
- How to apply decorative trims

WHAT YOU'LL NEED...............

- ⅝ yd. (0.6 m) lightweight woven fabric for skirt
- ½ yd. (0.5 m) lightweight contrasting fabric for pockets, waistband, and ties
- Lightweight fusible interfacing, 2″ × 19″ (5.1 × 48.3 cm)
- Matching all-purpose thread
- 1 package of wide rick rack
- Glue stick

How to Sew an Apron

1 Prepare the fabric (page 41). Lay out the fabric in a single layer. Using a carpenter's square or quilter's ruler, measure and mark out the rectangles listed below. Mark the skirt piece on one fabric; mark the waistband, pockets, and ties on the other fabric. Do not use a selvage as one of the sides. Cut out the pieces.

(continued)

Dimensions for Apron Pieces

Skirt	20″ long x 30″ wide (50.8 x 76.2 cm)
2 pockets	8½″ long x 7½″ wide (21.6 x 19.2 cm)
Waistband	4½″ x 20″ (11.4 x 50.8 cm)
2 ties	4½″ x 28″ (11.4 x 71.1 cm)
Waistband interfacing	2″ x 19″ (5.1 x 48.3 cm)

How to Sew an Apron *continued*

2 Fold upper edge of once pocket piece 1" (2.5 cm) to the wrong side and press. Unfold the edge and turn the raw edge in to meet the pressed fold; press again. Then refold the edge, and press again, forming a double-fold facing. Repeat for the other pocket.

3 Turn the facing to the right side of the pocket, even with the bottom fold. Pin the layers together at the sides. Starting at the top of the pocket, stitch a ½" (1.3 cm) seam to the bottom of the facing on each side of the pocket, *back-stitching (p. 19)* at the beginning and end. *Trim the corners diagonally*. Trim the facing seam allowance to ¼" (6 mm)

4 Turn the facing to the inside. Using a point turner or similar tool, gently push out the corners to square them off. Press the top fold; the facing should be ½" (1.3 cm) wide. Fold in the sides ½" (1.3 cm), and press. To square the bottom corners, turn under ½" (1.3 cm) on the bottom, and press.

> ### QUICK REFERENCE
> *Trim the upper corners diagonally.* This minimizes the excess bulk to form a smoother corner when the piece is turned back to the inside.

5 Find the ⅜" (1 cm) seam guide on the throat plate. For easier guiding, mark this distance from the needle on the machine bed, using tape. Topstitch the upper edge of the pocket, guiding the fold along the tape mark and catching the facing in the stitches.

6 Cut rick rack the width of the pocket plus 1¼" (3.2 cm). Apply glue stick to the back of the rick rack. Place the rick rack over the facing stitching line, wrapping the ends to the underside of the pocket. Stitch down the center of the rick rack, backstitching at the sides of the pocket. Repeat for other pocket.

7 Place the pockets on the apron skirt 9½" (24.1 cm) from the long bottom edge and 6" (15.2 cm) from the sides. Make sure the pocket edges are parallel to the skirt edges. Pin the sides and bottom edges of the pockets to the skirt, inserting the pins perpendicular to the pocket edges.

(continued)

How to Sew an Apron continued

8 With a pencil or erasable fabric marker, draw
a small *triangle* in each upper corner of each
pocket, ⅛" (3 mm) from the top and side edges.
Place the skirt under the presser foot with the top
of the pocket toward you, aligning the needle to
start sewing at the lowest point of the triangle.
Stitch forward two stitches, then backstitch two
stitches. Now stitch diagonally to the top, pivot,
and stitch a few stitches across the top of the
triangle. Pivot again so the needle is now aligned
to stitch down the side of the pocket. Edgestitch
around the sides and the bottom of the pocket,
and finish with the triangle on the opposite corner,
again backstitching two stitches.

TIP Apron pockets are used frequently. Stitching triangles at the top corners reinforces them better
than merely backstitching, which can put more
strain on the skirt fabric beneath the pocket.

9 Turn under the lower edge of the skirt 2"
(5.1 cm) and press. Unfold the edge and turn
the raw edge in to meet the pressed fold; press
again. Refold the edge, forming a 1" (2.5 cm) **double-fold hem**. Insert pins perpendicular to
the folds.

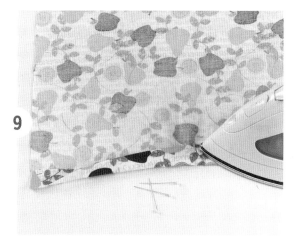

10 At the bottom corner of the skirt, turn
the hem to the right side, keeping the
inner fold in place. Pin the layers together at the
sides. Stitch a 1" (2.5 cm) seam across the hem,
backstitching at the beginning and end. Trim the
corner diagonally. Turn the corner right side out.
Repeat for other side.

11 Fold and press ½" (1.3 cm) double-fold hems in the skirt sides, making the first fold 1" (2.5 cm) deep. Insert pins perpendicular to the folds.

12 Place the skirt, right side down, under the presser foot with the bulk of the fabric to the left of the machine. Beginning at the top of the side hem, stitch along the inner fold, removing pins as you come to them. Pivot at the top fold of the bottom hem, and stitch along the hem fold to the opposite side. Pivot again, and stitch along the inner fold of the other side hem to the skirt top.

13 Cut rick rack the width of the skirt plus 1¼" (3.2 cm). Apply rickrack over the stitching line of the bottom hem, following step 6.

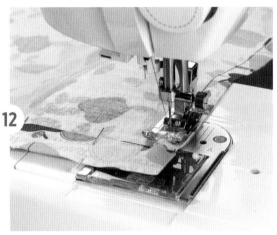

14 Set your machine to sew long straight stitches. Beginning at one side hem, baste a scant ½" (1.3 cm) from the top edge of the skirt. Stitch from the right side of the fabric. Stop stitching at the opposite side hem. Stitch another row of long stitches ¼" (6 mm) closer to the edge. Leave thread tails at each end. Set the skirt aside.

(continued)

QUICK REFERENCE

Double-fold hem. Double-fold hems are made with two folds of equal depths, encasing the cut edge in the crease of the outer fold. Pressing the first fold to the total hem depth allows you to be more accurate in turning and pressing.

How to Sew an Apron continued

15 Fold a tie lengthwise, with right sides together and raw edges even. Insert pins perpendicular to the edges. Stitch ½" (1.3 cm) seam across one end of the tie and the long edge. Trim corners diagonally. Repeat for the other tie. Turn the ties right side out (p. 139). Press. Topstitch ⅛" (3 mm) from outside edges. Set the ties aside.

16 Press the waistband in half lengthwise, and unfold. Place the interfacing strip, fusible side down, on the wrong side of the waistband, aligning one long edge to the center crease and centering the strip lengthwise. Fuse the interfacing in place.

17 Press under ⅜" (1 cm) on the long unfused edge of the waistband. Mark the cut edge of the waistband ½" (1.3 cm) from each end. Then divide the waistband into four equal parts, and mark, using chalk pencil or erasable marker. Also divide the upper edge of the skirt into four equal parts, and mark.

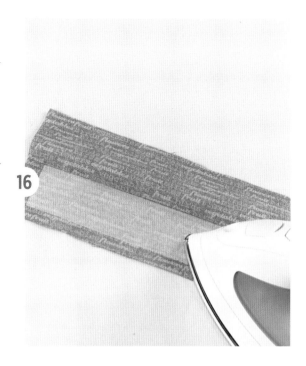

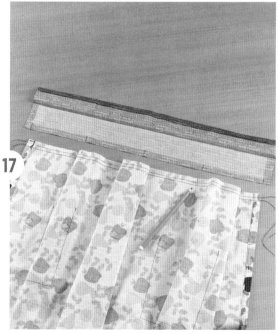

18 With right sides together, pin the cut edge of the waistband to the upper edge of the skirt, matching quarter marks. Insert pins from the skirt side. At one end, grasp both of the bobbin threads, and pull on them with equal tension, sliding the fabric along the thread to gather it.

19 Keep pulling on the bobbin threads, gathering the fabric, and distributing the gathers evenly between the pins on half of the waistband. When the skirt fabric is gathered up to fit that half, secure the bobbin threads by winding them in a figure eight around the end pin.

20 Pull the bobbin threads from the other end to gather the remaining half; secure the threads. Distribute all the gathered fabric evenly along the waistband, inserting pins frequently to hold the fabric in place.

(continued)

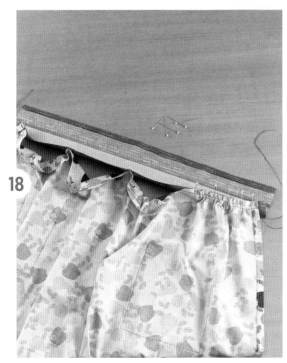

How to Sew an Apron *continued*

21 Reset the stitch length for 10 to 12 stitches per inch, which is 2 to 2.5 mm. Place the fabric under the presser foot, the waistband on the bottom. Stitch the waist seam ½" (1.3 cm) from the raw edges. Keep the gathers even and remove pins as you come to them.

22 Trim the seam allowances just above the gathering stitches.

23 Turn the seam allowance toward the waistband, and press lightly with the tip of the iron. Avoid pressing creases into the gathers.

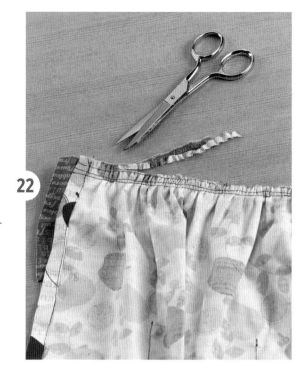

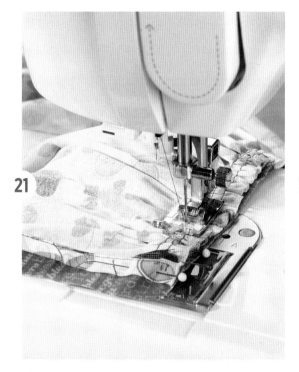

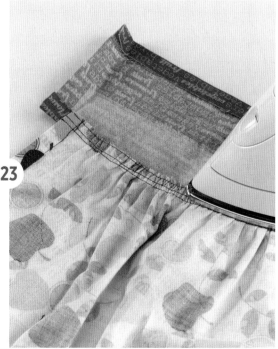

24 Pin the ties to the short ends of the waistband, right sides together. Fold the center crease of the waistband in the opposite direction over the ties, right sides together. Stitch a ½" (1.3 cm) seam across each end of the waistband. Trim the seams and clip the corners diagonally.

25 Turn the waistband right side out, encasing the raw ends of the ties. Press. The folded edge should extend down over the seam on the wrong side. From the right side, pin in the ditch of the waistband seam, catching the folded edge on the back.

TIP Be sure to keep the seam allowance turned up as it was pressed. Check to be sure the folded edge of the waistband is pinned at a consistent depth and lies flat.

26 *Stitch in the ditch (p. 74)* of the seam from the right side of the skirt, backstitching at the ends of the waistband and removing pins as you come to them. Be careful not to catch the ties in the stitching.

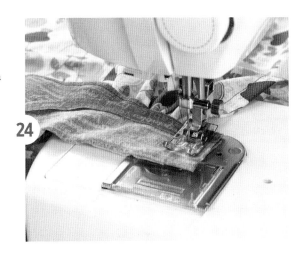

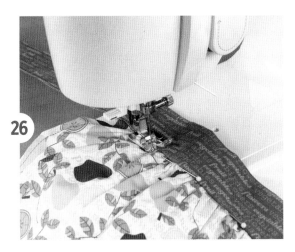

Unlined Jackets

Collarless jackets are versatile additions to any wardrobe. Those that are loose-fitting and unlined, with drop-shoulder styling and patch pockets, are easy to make. Look for a pattern that includes pieces for front, back, sleeve, front facing, back facing, and pocket. These directions are for square bottom front corners. If your pattern has round corners, pay close attention to the pattern directions when attaching the facing (step 11) and hemming the lower edge (steps 24 to 27).

As with any other project, the fabric of your jacket will determine whether it will be more suitable for casual, business, or dress. Cotton, cotton blends, and denim would be good choices to wear with jeans or casual slacks and skirts. Wool, wool blends, linen, and rayon work for business or dress. When you're feeling really confident, you might even consider making a jacket of suit-weight silk, like the one at left.

WHAT YOU'LL LEARN. . . . .

- How to sew a drop-shoulder sleeve
- How to sew a patch pocket
- How to apply fusible interfacing
- How to sew neck and front facings

WHAT YOU'LL NEED. . . . .

- Jacket pattern; unlined, loose-fitting
- Fabric for jacket (check pattern for amount)
- Matching all-purpose thread
- Lightweight fusible interfacing (check pattern for amount)
- Buttons

How to Sew an Unlined Jacket

1 Prepare the fabric (page 41). Lay out the pattern pieces (page 52), and cut out (page 56) all but the facings. Fuse interfacing to the wrong side of the fabric for the facings, ***following the manufacturer's directions (p. 63)***. Then cut out the facings. Transfer any necessary marks (page 57).

(continued)

How to Sew an Unlined Jacket continued

2 Turn under the top edge of the pocket ¼" (6 mm); press. To finish the edge, set your machine for a zigzag stitch of medium length and width. Stitch close to the folded edge, so that the right-hand swing of the needle just clears the fold.

3 Turn the upper edge of the pocket (the facing) to the outside on the foldline; pin at the sides. Starting at the top of the pocket, stitch a ⅝" (1.5 cm) seam to the bottom of the facing on each side of the pocket, *backstitching (p. 19)* at the beginning and end. Trim the facing seam allowance to ⅜" (1 cm). Trim the upper corners diagonally.

4 Turn the facing to the inside. Using a point turner or similar tool, gently push out the corners to square them off. Press the top fold. If the pocket has square bottom corners, turn under ⅝" (1.5 cm) on the bottom, and press. Then repeat for the side edges.

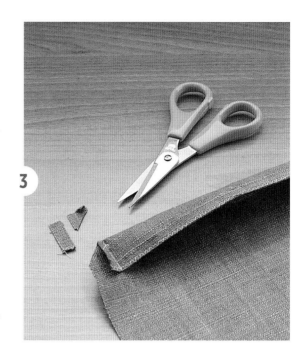

5 Set your sewing machine for a straight stitch of 10 to 12 stitches per inch, which is 2 to 2.5 mm. Measure the finished width of the facing; subtract ⅛" (3 mm). Mark this distance from the needle on the machine bed, using tape. Topstitch the upper edge of the pocket, guiding the fold along the tape mark and catching the facing in the stitches.

6 Repeat steps 2 to 5 for the other pocket. Place the pockets on the jacket front, matching the upper corners to the markings transferred from the pattern. Pin them securely in place, **inserting the pins perpendicular to the edges (p. 19)**. Edgestitch around the sides and bottom of the pockets, backstitching at both upper corners. Stop with the needle down in the fabric to pivot at each corner. **Remove the pins as you come to them (p. 19)**.

(continued)

How to Sew an Unlined Jacket *continued*

7 Pin the jacket fronts to the jacket back at the shoulders, with right sides together, aligning the cut edges and matching any notches. Insert the pins perpendicular to the edges.

8 Stitch the seams, guiding the cut edges along the ⅝" (1.5 cm) seam allowance guide. Press the seams flat; then press them open.

9 Sew the front facings to the back facing at the shoulders as in steps 7 and 8. Trim the seam allowances to ¼" (6 mm). Finish the inner, unnotched edges of the front facings and the lower edge of the back facing (arrows) as in step 2.

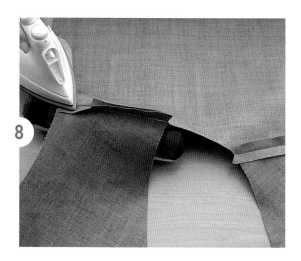

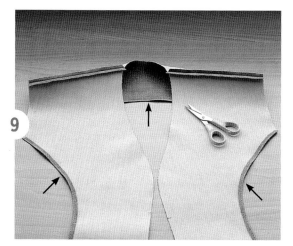

10 Pin the facing to the jacket, right sides together, aligning the cut edges. Match the shoulder seams and all notches. At the shoulders, insert a pin in the wells of the seams, to keep them aligned.

11 Stitch the facing to the jacket, guiding the cut edges along the ⅝" (1.5 cm) seam allowance guide. Stitch continuously from one lower edge, around the neckline, to the opposite lower edge; backstitch a few stitches at the beginning and end. Remove the pins as you come to them, and keep the shoulder seam allowances open flat.

12 Grade the seam allowances by trimming the jacket neckline seam allowance to ⅜" (1 cm) and the facing seam allowance to ¼" (6 mm). Clip into the neckline seam allowance every ½" (1.3 cm), clipping up to, but not through, the stitches. Clipping allows the facing to turn smoothly to the inside and lie flat.

(continued)

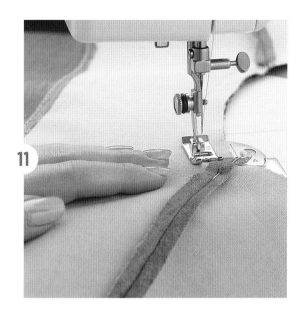

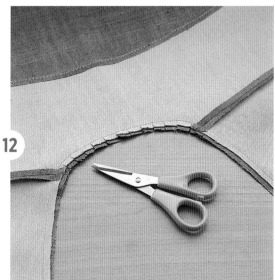

How to Sew an Unlined Jacket continued

13 Press the seam allowances flat; then press them toward the facing. With the right side up, place the facing (A) under the presser foot, so the needle is aligned to enter the fabric just to the right of the seam at the lower left front; the jacket (B) extends off the left of the machine bed. Keeping the seam allowance turned toward the facing (arrows), stitch all around the fronts and neckline very close to the seam. You will be stitching through the facing and the seam allowance, but not through the jacket. This step, called understitching, helps the facing lie flat.

TIP Along the curve of the neckline, keep the facing lying flat, allowing the jacket to "bunch up" to the left of the curve. Stitch, following the curve of the facing. The clipped seam allowance will "fan out" underneath the facing.

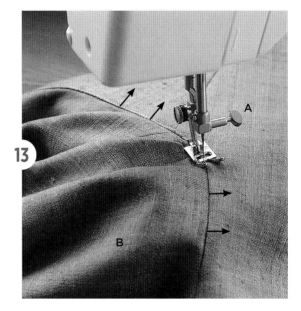

14 Turn the facing to the inside; press. Align the shoulder seams, and smooth them out to the sleeve edge. Pin the facing to the sleeve edge, inserting the pins perpendicular to the edge. Set your machine for long straight stitches. Baste the facings to the sleeve edges.

TIP Some jacket patterns have facings that do not extend all the way to the sleeve edge. Align the shoulder seam allowances, and *stitch in the ditch (p. 57)* to secure the facing to the jacket.

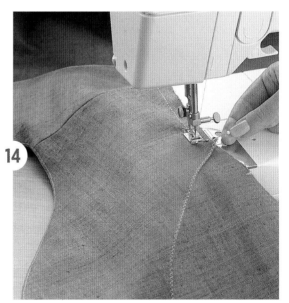

15 Pin the sleeve to the jacket, with right sides together. Align the cut edges, and match the notches. You probably also have a mark on the sleeve edge that aligns to the jacket shoulder seam. Count the notches to be sure you are pinning the correct sleeve. Pin frequently from the jacket side, easing the sleeve to fit smoothly.

16 Place the jacket under the presser foot, with the sleeve underneath. Stitch the seam, guiding the edges along the ⅝" (1.5 cm) seam allowance guide. Remove the pins as you come to them.

17 Check from the sleeve side, to be sure there are no puckers. If there are any, clip the stitches, using a seam ripper, and remove the stitches on either side of the pucker far enough to smooth it out; restitch.

(continued)

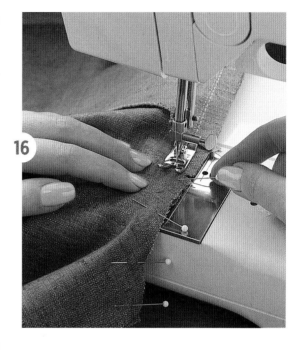

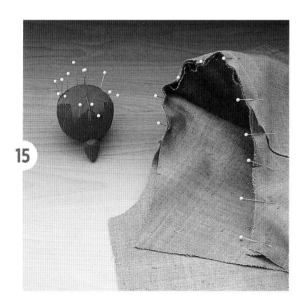

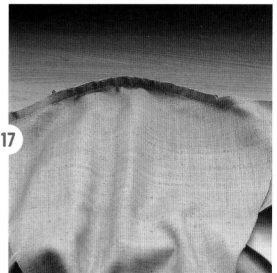

How to Sew an Unlined Jacket continued

18 Stitch a second line in the seam allowances, ¼" (6 mm) from the first stitching line, from the notches to each end. Trim the seam allowances in this area close to the second stitching line.

19 Repeat steps 15 to 18 for the opposite sleeve. Set your machine for a medium-length, medium-width zigzag stitch. For each sleeve, finish the seam allowance edges together, stitching so that the right swing of the needle just clears the fabric edge. Press the seam allowances toward the sleeves.

20 Pin the jacket front to the jacket back, right sides together, along the side seams and extending on to the underarm sleeve seams. Match notches, and align the sleeve seams. Insert the pins perpendicular to the edges.

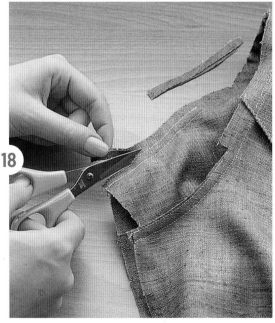

21 Stitch ⅝" (1.5 cm) seam from the bottom of one side continuously to the end of the sleeve. Keep the underarm seam allowances turned toward the sleeve. Repeat for the opposite side.

22 Finish the side and underarm seam allowances as in step 2. Press the seam allowances flat; then press them open.

TIP Press the seam allowances open over a seam roll to prevent imprinting the seam allowance edges onto the right side of the jacket and to make it easier to press the sleeve seams open.

(continued)

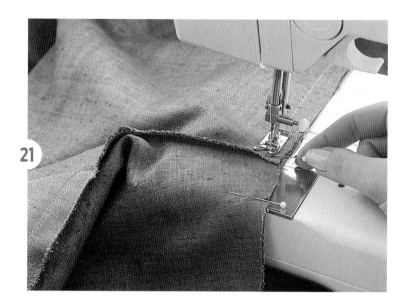

How to Sew an Unlined Jacket *continued*

23 Finish the lower edge of the jacket as in step 2. Repeat for the lower edges of the sleeves. Turn under the remaining hem allowances on the sleeves, and press, using a seam roll or sleeve board (page 31). Slipstitch (page 22) the hems to the jacket.

24 Place the jacket on your ironing board, wrong side up; open the front facings. Turn under the remaining hem allowance on the lower edge, including the facings; press.

25 Unfold the lower edge. Turn the jacket over, and turn the facing to the outside, aligning the lower edges. Pin, keeping the facing seam allowances turned toward the facing. Stitch the facing to the jacket, stitching in the well of the pressed fold. Repeat for the opposite side.

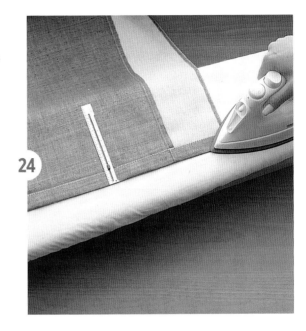

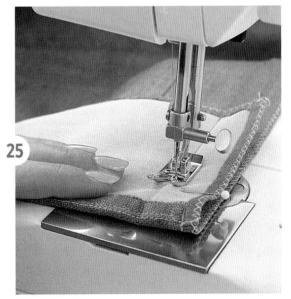

26 Trim the facing seam allowance to within ¼" (6 mm) of the stitches. Trim the corner diagonally, to within ⅛" (3 mm) of the corner stitch. Repeat for the opposite side. Turn the facings to the inside, and press.

27 Refold the remaining hem, and pin. Slipstitch the hem to the jacket. At the fronts, slipstitch the facings to the hem.

28 Topstitch ⅜" (1 cm) from the edges along the fronts and neckline of the jacket, if desired. If your jacket has buttons, transfer the buttonhole placement marks from your pattern to the right jacket front. Make buttonholes, following the directions in your sewing machine owner's manual. Transfer the button placement marks to the left front. Sew buttons as on page 23.

26

27

28

Sewing Home Décor

Although there are many commercial patterns available for sewing home décor items, the projects in this section do not require patterns. Most of the pieces you need to cut are squares and rectangles, which can be easily measured and marked out on the fabric for cutting. The directions will tell you exactly what sizes to cut the necessary pieces, and often include an illustration to help you plan the cutting lines on your fabric.

The projects are arranged in order from easiest to most complicated, and different sewing skills are taught in each project. While you may want to jump right in and sew a quilted placemat, it is well worth your time to at least read through the previous projects and study the techniques introduced in each one.

Raw-edge Flange Pillows

A raw-edge flange pillow is a great first sewing project, requiring only very basic sewing skills and knowledge. This small 12" (30.5 cm) square pillow looks larger because of its flange, a border of flat fabric extending beyond the stitching line, around the outer edge of the pillow. We have selected synthetic fleece for this pillow project, because it is an easy fabric to work with; it does not ravel, and its natural loft will hide your stitches. In other words, don't be concerned if your stitching line wavers a bit; your pillow will still be gorgeous! You may recognize fleece as a popular fabric for ready-to-wear mittens, hats, and jackets. Imagine wonderful, cozy fleece pillows for a casual den or a child's bedroom. We have planned a 2½" (6.5 cm) flange around the pillow, so 5" (12.5 cm) must be added to the pillow dimensions.

WHAT YOU'LL LEARN...............

- How to cut out fabric, following the fabric grainline
- How to mark fabric
- How to match and pin edges together
- How to sew a straight line and pivot at corners
- That you can sew a great-looking pillow!

WHAT YOU'LL NEED................

- ½ yd. (0.5 m) synthetic fleece fabric, 45" or 60" (115 or 152.5 cm) wide
- Air-erasable marking pen or narrow masking tape
- Thread in a color to match the fabric
- 12" (30.5 cm) square knife-edge pillow form

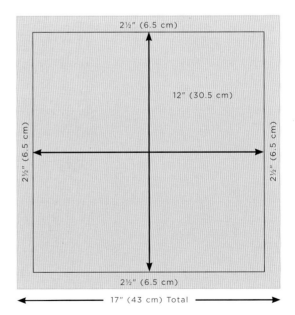

How to Sew a Raw-Edge Flange Pillow

1 Cut two 17" (43 cm) squares of fabric. Be sure
to make your cuts on the fabric grainlines
(page 38).

TIP Make yourself a paper pattern, and pin it to the
fabric; then simply cut around it. This is easier
than marking lines on the fleece.

2 Mark a square on the pillow front 2½"
(6.5 cm) in from the four sides; this will
be your stitching line. You can do this with an
air-erasable marking pen, or place narrow
strips of masking tape with one edge along the
stitching line.

3 Pin the pillow front to the pillow back, with
the right sides of the fabric facing out (wrong
sides together). Insert the pins along the marked
stitching line, inserting pins perpendicular to the
line. This will make it easy to remove the pins as
you sew. Leave a 7" (18 cm) section on one side
unpinned. This is where you will leave an opening
for inserting the pillow.

4 Place the pinned fabric under the presser foot, so that the opening will be just behind the presser foot. Begin sewing, stitching over the line if you marked it with a pen, or stitching right next to the tape, if you marked it with tape. Remove pins as you come to them; stitching over pins is hazardous to the health of your sewing machine. Stop sewing at the first corner, leaving the needle down in the fabric. (Turn the handwheel until the needle is down.)

5 Raise the presser foot and turn the fabric a quarter turn. Lower the presser foot and continue sewing to the next corner. Repeat this pivot procedure at each corner. Stop stitching when you reach the last pin, leaving the opening unstitched. *Remove the fabric from the machine*.

TIP Relax your shoulders and rest your elbows on the table next to your machine as you sew. Guide the fabric with your fingertips, moving your hands from the wrists. Let your machine work while you have fun!

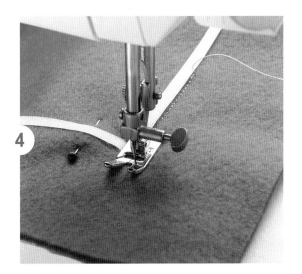

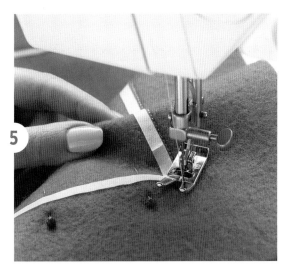

(continued)

QUICK REFERENCE

Air-erasable marking pen. This innovative tool marks the fabric with a fine colored line (usually purple or magenta). The "ink" evaporates and disappears within 48 hours, so you will want to mark your fabric just before you sew. Always test first on a scrap of fabric to make sure the marks will completely disappear.

Removing fabric from the machine. When you finish a stitching line, always stop with the needle out of the fabric and the take-up lever in the highest position. (Some newer machines automatically do this for you.) Raise the presser foot; pull the fabric to the side or toward the back. Clip the threads, leaving several inches of thread extending from the needle and bobbin.

How to Sew a Raw-Edge Flange Pillow *continued*

6 Fold or bunch the pillow form and insert it through the opening. Allow the first and last stitches to loosen, if necessary, so the fleece is not damaged. Push the form away from the opening and pin the opening together, making sure the raw edges are aligned. Gently pull the thread tails to snug the loosened stitches.

7 Place the pillow back under the presser foot so that the opening is lined up in front of the presser foot and the end of the stitching line is visible just in front of the foot. Sew the opening closed, overlapping the ends of the previous stitching line by about 1" (2.5 cm). Remove the pillow from the machine and clip all the threads close to the fleece. If you marked your stitching line with tape, it is now safe to remove it!

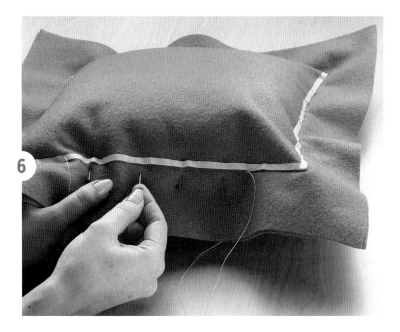

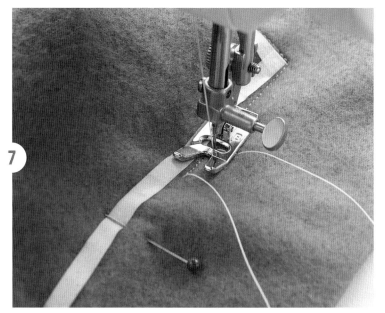

Raw-edge Flange with a Twist

Use synthetic suede, such as Ultrasuede for a luxurious formal look. To make stitching on synthetic suede easier, add one drop of silicone lubricant to the spool of thread before filling the bobbin and threading the machine. Also, apply a drop of lubricant to the needle, the bottom of the presser foot, and the throat plate.

Select a coarse, even-weave fabric such as this silk. Take special care to cut and sew the pillow following the grainlines. Stitch again ¾" (2 cm) beyond the first stitching line. Pull threads to fray the flange.

Cut fringe into the flange edges of a fleece or Ultrasuede pillow. Mark cutting guidelines ½" (1.3 cm) apart along each edge. Cut to within ⅛" (3 mm) of the stitches.

Knife-edge Pillows

The knife-edge pillow is probably the most versatile style for decorating your home. There are no limits to the variations you can create, not only in size, color, and texture, but also in added details that give your pillow a personal touch. The directions that follow are for a knife-edge pillow that is 14" (35.5 cm) square. For your first knife-edge pillow, we recommend a firmly woven mediumweight fabric.

Ready-made knife-edge pillow inserts come in a wide selection of sizes, including 12", 14", 16", 18", 20", 24", and 30" (30.5, 35.5, 40.5, 46, 51, 61, and 76 cm) squares and a 12" × 16" (30.5 × 40.5 cm) rectangle. By adapting these cutting instructions, you can sew a cover for any size pillow insert. You can also use these instructions to sew your own pillow inserts in any size you like, stuffing them to a plumpness that pleases you.

WHAT YOU'LL LEARN . . . .

- How to **backstitch (p. 19)**
- How to set and press seams
- Tricks for sewing perfect corners
- How to slipstitch (page 22) an opening closed by hand

WHAT YOU'LL NEED . . . .

- 14" (35.5 cm) square pillow form
- ½ yd. (0.5 m) of fabric
- Matching thread
- Hand-sewing needle

How to Sew a Knife-edge Pillow

1 Cut two 15" (38 cm) squares of fabric, aligning the sides to the fabric grainlines (page 38). A ½" (1.3 cm) seam allowance is needed on each side, so 1" (2.5 cm) is added to each dimension of the **desired finished size (p. 126)**.

(continued)

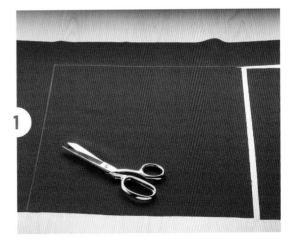

How to Sew a Knife-Edge Pillow continued

2 Place the pillow front over the pillow back, right sides together, and align all four edges. Pin the layers together near the outer edges, **inserting the pins perpendicular to the edges (p. 19)**. In the center of one side, leave a 7" (18 cm) opening unpinned.

3 Place the fabric under the presser foot, just ahead of the opening. Align the cut edges of the fabric to the ½" (1.3 cm) **seam allowance guide (p. 19)** on the bed of your machine. Remove the pin that marks the opening, before lowering the presser foot.

QUICK REFERENCE

Desired finished size. To make a knife-edge pillow of a different size, simply cut your fabric 1" (2.5 cm) larger in both directions than the desired finished size of your pillow. Cut 17" (43 cm) squares for a 16" (40.5 cm) pillow; cut 13" × 19" (33 × 48.5 cm) rectangles for a 12" × 18" (30.5 × 46 cm) pillow.

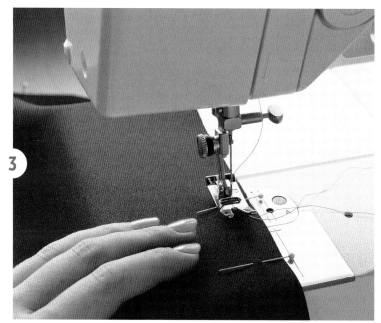

4 Backstitch three or four
stitches; stop. Then, stitching forward, stitch the seam on
all four sides, pivoting with the
needle down at the corners. End
the seam at the opposite side of
the opening; backstitch three or
four stitches.

5 *Remove the fabric from
the machine (p. 121)*. Trim
the threads close to the fabric.
Press the seams flat to set the
stitching line in the fabric. This
may seem unnecessary, but
it really does give you a better-looking seam in the end.

TIP Most machines have a
handy thread cutter located
within a few inches (centimeters) of the presser foot. By using
this thread cutter, you are also pulling
enough thread through the needle and
up from the bobbin to help you prevent a thread jam at the start of your
next seam.

(continued)

How to Sew a Knife-Edge Pillow continued

6 Turn back the top seam allowance, and press, applying light pressure with tip of the iron down the crease of the seam. In the area of the opening, turn back and press the top seam allowance ½" (1.3 cm).

7 Turn the cover over; turn back and press the remaining opening seam allowance.

8 To turn a **perfect corner**, fold in the seam allowances from one edge, and then fold in the seam allowances from the adjacent edge over them. Slip four fingers through the pillow opening and pinch the folded corner between your thumb and one finger. Turn that corner through the opening. Repeat with the other three corners. Your pillow cover has now been turned right side out.

9 Compress and insert the pillow form. Align the pressed edges of the opening, and pin the opening closed. Thread a hand needle and tie a knot in the end.

10 Slipstitch the opening closed, following the instructions on page 22.

instructions on page 22.

QUICK REFERENCE

Perfect corner. The corners of your pillow should be sharply squared, not rounded. To improve the appearance of a slightly rounded corner, you can push a pointed utensil into the corner from inside the pillow cover to force the stitches out to the corner. An inexpensive specialty tool, called a point turner (page 33), works well; or you can use a large knitting needle, a ballpoint pen with the inkball retracted, or something similar. Use light pressure, though, so that you don't punch a hole in the corner.

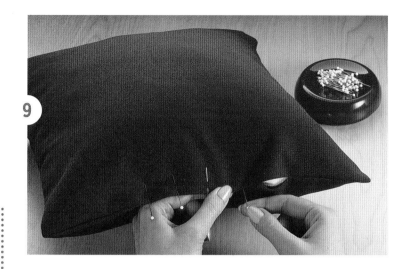

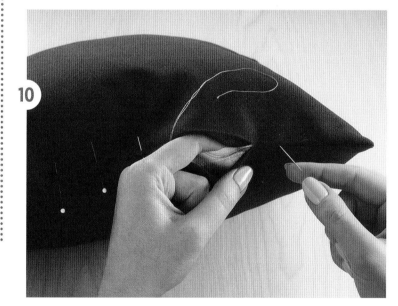

Zipper Closures

Pillows that get tossed around, leaned upon, and slid across the floor need occasional cleaning. A zipper closure sewn into a seam makes it much easier to remove and reinsert the pillow form. Any of the knife-edge-style pillows can be made with a zipper closure. Cut the fabric and prepare the pillow front and back according to the directions in the project. Then follow these directions to complete the pillow.

Purchase a conventional polyester coil zipper (not a separating style) to match your fabric, in the size indicated in the chart below.

How to Sew a Zipper Closure

1 Place the pillow front over the pillow back, right sides together. Pin the side that will have the zipper. Center the zipper alongside the pinned edges, and mark the seam allowances just above and below the **zipper stops (p. 132)**.

> **TIP** For best results, select a side that was cut on the lengthwise grain of the fabric. The lengthwise grain is more stable and will have less tendency to stretch as you sew.

2 Stitch a ½" (1.3 cm) seam from the upper edge to the mark, **backstitching (p. 19)** at the beginning and the end. Repeat at the lower edge. Leave the center section open.

(continued)

Zipper	Pillow
7" (18 cm)	12" to 14" (30.5 to 35.5 cm)
9" (23 cm)	16" to 18" (40.5 to 46 cm)
12" (30.5 cm)	20" (51 cm) or larger

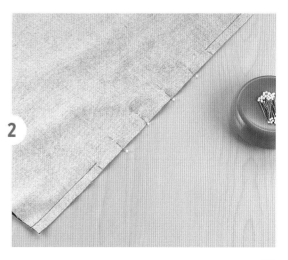

How to Sew a Zipper Closure *continued*

3 **Machine-baste** on the seamline between the marks. Clip the basting stitches every 2" (5 cm) with a seam ripper. This will make the stitches easier to remove later

4 Press the seam flat; then press the seam allowances open. Finish the seam allowances with a zigzag stitch (page 21).

TIP If your fabric is loosely woven or tends to ravel easily, repeated washings could make the seam allowances ravel away and ruin your pillow. As a preventative measure, take the time to finish all of the seam allowances.

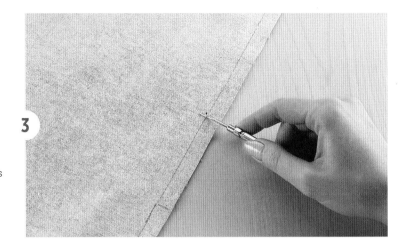

QUICK REFERENCE

Zipper stops. Tiny metal bars are attached to the top and bottom of the zipper coil to prevent the zipper slide from sliding right off the end. On a conventional zipper, there is one wide stop at the bottom of the zipper and separate smaller stops at the top.

Machine-baste. Set the machine for the longest straight stitch possible. This stitching is temporary and will be easily removed later.

Basting tape. This narrow tape is adhesive on both sides. As the tape comes off the roll, one side is sticky. After placing it on the zipper, remove the protective backing, exposing the other sticky side. Basting tape need not be removed after the zipper is stitched in place.

5 Apply **basting tape** to the right side of the zipper tape, running it along both outer edges.

6 Place the zipper facedown over the seam, with the zipper coil directly over the basted part of the seamline and the pull tab turned down. The zipper coil should be centered between the backstitched areas. Press with your fingers to secure the zipper to the seam allowances.

(continued)

5

6

How to Sew a Zipper Closure *continued*

7 Spread the pillow pieces flat, right side up. Insert pins in the seamline, just above and below the zipper stops. Cut ½" (1.3 cm) transparent tape to fit between the pins; place it down the center of the seamline.

8 Attach the zipper foot and adjust it to the left of the needle. If your zipper foot is not adjustable, adjust the needle to the right of the foot. Stitch along the outer edge of the tape, stitching across one end, down one side, and across the other end; pivot at the corners.

9 Adjust the zipper foot to the right of the needle or adjust your needle to the left of the foot. Stitch over the previous stitches at one end, down the opposite side, and over the stitches at the other end. Clip the threads.

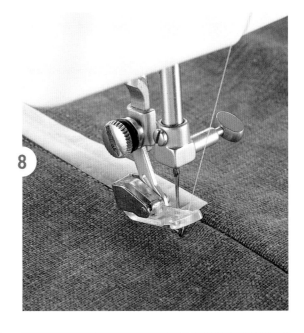

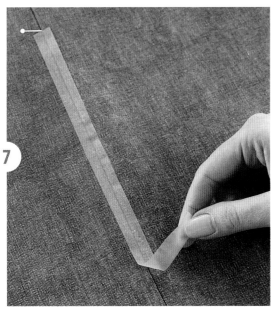

10 Remove the tape. Carefully remove the machine basting in the seamline, using a seam ripper.

11 Open the zipper. Pin the pillow front and back, right sides together, along the three remaining sides. Stitch ½" (1.3 cm) seam; press. Turn the pillow cover right side out and insert the pillow form through the zipper opening.

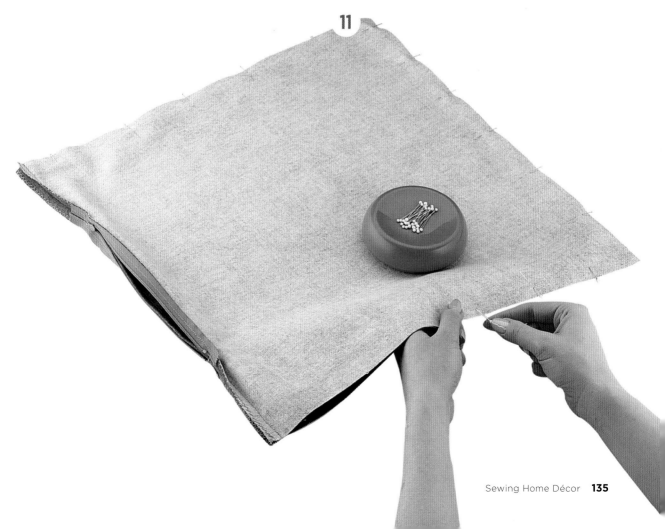

Tie-tab Pillowcases

This is a unique way to dress up a ho-hum knife-edge pillow. Slip it inside a colorful pillowcase, tied with narrow fabric ties. Create your own cheerful combo, beginning with a basic knife-edge pillow (page 125). Then sew a pillowcase, following these directions. Just think of all the interesting variations and color combinations you can create.

WHAT YOU'LL LEARN . . . .

- How to make fabric ties
- How to sew a facing

WHAT YOU'LL NEED . . . .

- Knife-edge pillow in desired size
- Coordinating fabric for the pillowcase, amount determined by the pillow size
- Thread to match the fabric

How to Sew a Tie-tab Pillowcase

1 Cut two rectangles of fabric for the front and back of the pillowcase, with the length equal to the length of the knife-edge pillow plus 1" (2.5 cm), and the width equal to the finished width of the knife-edge pillow. Cut a 2" (5 cm) strip of fabric for the facing with the length equal to two times the length of the pillow plus 1" (2.5 cm). Remember to follow the grainlines (page 38). Cut twelve strips of fabric for the ties, 12" (30.5 cm) long and 1¼" (3.2 cm) wide. Cut them with the length running on the lengthwise grain.

TIP The length here refers to the pillow from top to bottom, if you intend to place the ties at the pillow side. If you want the ties at the top, then length refers to the side-to-side measurement.

(continued)

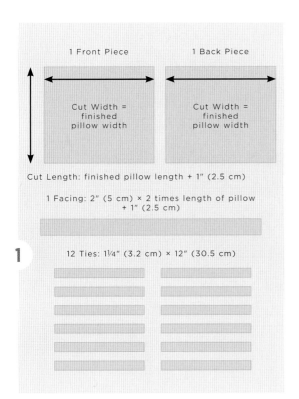

1 Front Piece   1 Back Piece

Cut Width = finished pillow width

Cut Width = finished pillow width

Cut Length: finished pillow length + 1" (2.5 cm)

1 Facing: 2" (5 cm) × 2 times length of pillow + 1" (2.5 cm)

12 Ties: 1¼" (3.2 cm) × 12" (30.5 cm)

1

How to Sew a Tie-tab Pillowcase continued

2 Place the pillowcase front over the back, right sides together, and align all four edges. Pin the layers together near three outer edges, leaving the fourth side (the side where the ties will go) open. Stitch ½" (1.3 cm) seams along the three pinned sides, **backstitching (p. 19)** at the beginning and end.

3 Press the seams flat; then press them open. Turn the pillowcase right side out. Insert a point turner (page 33) or similar tool into the case to push the corners out gently, if necessary.

4 Pin two tie strips, right sides together, matching the raw edges. **Stitch ¼" (6 mm) seam** around the long edges and one short end. Repeat for the remaining five sets of ties.

3

2

4

5 *Trim the corners diagonally (p. 96). Turn the ties right side out.* Use a point turner or similar tool to push the corners out gently, if necessary. Press the ties flat.

6 Pin the ties to the right side of the pillowcase along the unstitched edge, aligning the raw edges. Position one tie at the center of each side. Position the remaining four ties 2½" (6.5 cm) from the seams. Stitch ⅜" (1 cm) from the end of each tie, stitching only through one pillow layer.

(continued)

QUICK REFERENCE

Stitch ¼" (6 mm) seam. Sometimes the distance from the needle tip to the edge of the presser foot is ¼" (6 mm). If this isn't true for your machine, measure the distance and take note of the location on the presser foot or bed of the machine that measures an exact ¼" (6 mm).

Turn the ties right side out. There are special tools for turning narrow tubes inside out, including the FASTURN shown in the photo. Because this is a frequently required task in sewing, it is worth it to buy one of these tools. In a pinch, you can probably get the job done by working the fabric over the eraser end of a pencil, but it's much harder to do.

How to Sew a Tie-tab Pillowcase *continued*

7 Fold the facing strip, right sides together, matching the short ends. Stitch ½" (1.3 cm) seam across the short ends. Press the seam flat; then press it open.

8 Press under ½" (1.3 cm) along one edge of the facing. Pin the unpressed edge of the facing to the open edge of the pillowcase, right sides together. Align the seam of the facing to one seam of the pillowcase.

9 Stitch ½" (1.3 cm) seam around the opening. Press the seam flat; then press it open.

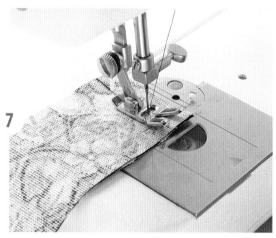

10 Press the facing to the inside of the pillowcase, with the seam on the opening edge. The ties will now extend out from the opening. Pin the facing in place. Stitch along the inner fold of the facing, removing the pins as you come to them.

11 Tuck the knife-edge pillow into the pillowcase, and tie the ties. Now pat yourself on the back. You've just made a great-looking pillow!

Baby Blanket

Blankets serve many purposes in the day-to-day routine of baby care. Most often they provide comfort, warmth, and security for little tykes. A blanket also provides a soft surface for rolling around on the floor or a make-do pad for a quick change when you're on the go. With easy-to-apply blanket binding and synthetic fleece fabric, you can sew up new blankets in a jiffy. Because the following method involves the use of fabric glue, you'll want to launder the finished blanket before you use it.

WHAT YOU'LL LEARN.............

- How to apply satin blanket binding
- The secret to sewing mitered corners
- The importance of careful pressing

WHAT YOU'LL NEED...............

- 1 yd. (0.95 m) synthetic fleece
- Satin blanket binding in color to match or coordinate with fabric
- Quilting ruler or carpenter's square
- Fabric glue stick (page 33)
- Thread to match blanket binding

How to Sew a Baby Blanket

1 Cut a rectangle of fabric 36" × 45" (91.5 × 115 cm). Use a quilting ruler or carpenter's square to ensure square corners. In the following steps, unroll the binding from the package as you need it, and don't cut it until step 7.

TIP Synthetic fleece is actually a knit fabric and is usually 60" (152.5 cm) wide. Avoid using either of the selvages as a side of your rectangle because they may be slightly stretched out of shape.

(continued)

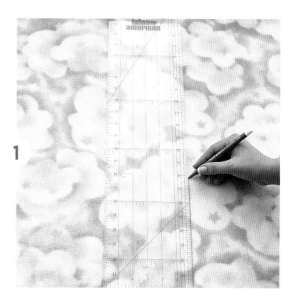

How to Sew a Baby Blanket continued

2 Beginning about 10" (25.5 cm) from one corner and working toward the corner in a clockwise direction, slip the blanket edge between the layers of the binding. Tuck the edge in as close as possible to the binding fold. Insert pins through all the layers, perpendicular to the edge. Space the pins about 2" (5 cm) apart with the heads outward.

TIP Be sure to keep the binding folded smooth and flat over the edge, so that the outer crease remains sharp. This will ensure that the finished binding edges on the front and back of the blanket are perfectly aligned.

3 Set the machine to sew a multistitch zigzag (page 21) at maximum width and 12 stitches per inch, which equals 2 mm. Place the blanket under the presser foot at the binding end, with the inner edge of the binding aligned to the **left side of the presser foot opening**. Stitch to the fabric edge, removing pins as you come to them. Stop, and **remove the fabric from the machine (p. 121)**.

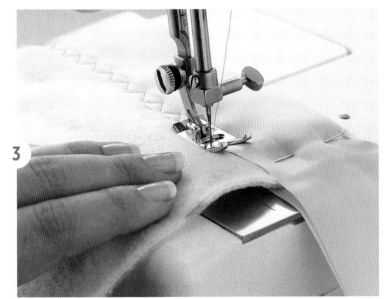

4 Take the blanket to the ironing board. Open out the binding at the corner, and fold it down along the next side, so that the fabric edge aligns to the binding fold. A 45° angle will form in the binding. Press the angle lightly with the tip of the iron.

5 Fold the binding closed so that the angled fold forms a mitered corner. The fold runs diagonally from the outer corner to the inner corner, matching up perfectly.

(continued)

4

5

QUICK REFERENCE

Left side of the presser foot opening. The opening in the center of the presser foot is more than wide enough to accommodate the widest stitch your machine can sew. Guide the fabric, keeping a tiny space between the binding edge and the left edge of the opening. The farthest left stitch of the needle should just stitch off the edge of the binding. Adjust the position slightly, if necessary.

How to Sew a Baby Blanket *continued*

6 Flip the blanket over and miter the back of the binding so that the diagonal fold on the back also lines up perfectly. Using a fabric glue stick, secure the folds in place. This is called *glue-basting*.

7 Encase and pin the blanket edge to the next corner. Place the blanket under the presser foot, aligning the inner corner of the miter to the left side of the presser foot opening. **Backstitch (p. 19)** two or three stitches. Stitch forward to the fabric edge at the next corner. Stop, and remove the blanket from the machine.

8 Repeat steps 4 to 7 for the remaining corners. On the side where you started, cut the binding 4" (10 cm) beyond the beginning. Open the fold; press under 2" (5 cm) at the end.

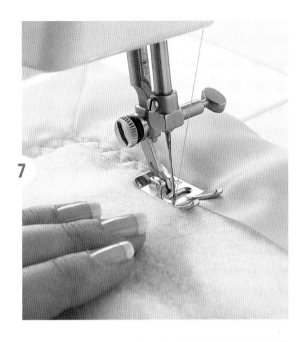

7

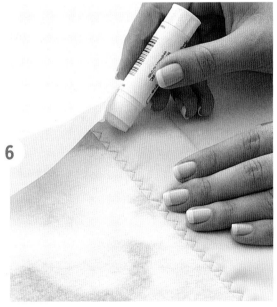

6

8

9 Refold and finish encasing and pinning the blanket edge. The folded end should overlap the cut end 2" (5 cm). Glue-baste the folded end in place. Stitch the last side, stitching about 1" (2.5 cm) beyond the overlap. Remove the blanket from the machine, and clip the threads.

10 *Reset the stitch length to 0*. Place the overlapped binding ends under the presser foot so that the fold is about ¼" (6 mm) ahead of the presser foot opening. Stitch in place until the needle has traveled from left to right at least twice. This tacking will keep the ends in place through many launderings.

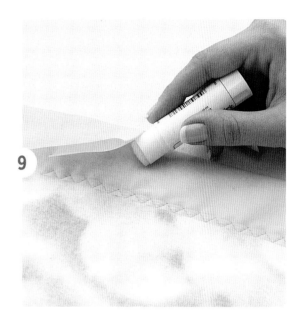

QUICK REFERENCE

Glue-basting. Use a fabric glue stick. This versatile product may become one of your favorite sewing tools. The temporary adhesive in a handy retractable tube can be applied in small dabs or continuous lines. It won't discolor the fabric and will wash out completely, if necessary.

Reset the stitch length to 0. The machine will still stitch side to side, as it is still set for multistitch-zigzag, but the fabric will not move forward.

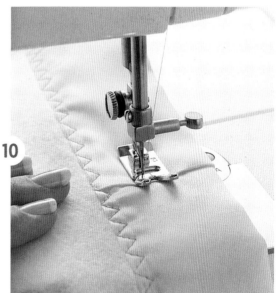

Nap-time Tote

When you take your baby for short visits, this convenient tote holds the essentials and zips open to provide a soft, cuddly surface for sleeping or playing. The tote is really a lined-to-the-edge square. A handy lined pocket running from front to back provides extra cushion through the center. Purchase prequilted fabric for the outer layer and cotton flannel for the lining. Be sure to preshrink both fabrics before cutting and sewing. Look for a 30" (76 cm) molded separating zipper in a color to coordinate with the fabric and lining.

WHAT YOU'LL LEARN. . . . .

- How to sew something that is lined to the edge
- How to use paper-backed fusible web (page 34)
- How to topstitch
- Zippers aren't as scary as you think!

WHAT YOU'LL NEED. . . . .

- Quilting ruler or carpenter's square for measuring and cutting
- 1¼ yd. (1.15 m) prequilted fabric
- 1¼ yd. (1.15 m) cotton flannel for lining
- Thread to match or blend with the fabrics
- Paper-backed fusible web, ⅜" (1 cm) wide
- 30" (76 cm) molded separating zipper
- Basting tape
- Point turner (page 33)

How to Sew a Nap-time Tote

1 Preshrink the fabric and lining. Using a quilting ruler or a carpenter's square, mark out a perfect 31" (78.5 cm) square on the prequilted fabric, for the tote. Also measure and mark a 13" × 27" (33 × 68.5 cm) rectangle for the pocket and two 4" × 15" (10 × 38 cm) rectangles for the handles. ***Do not use a selvage (p. 151)*** as one of the sides. Cut out the pieces. Using the square and the pocket piece as patterns, cut matching pieces from the lining fabric.

(continued)

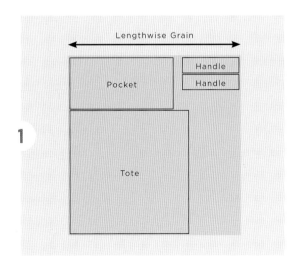

How to Sew a Nap-time Tote continued

2 Pin the lining over the pocket, right sides together, around the entire outer edge. ***Insert the pins perpendicular to the edges (p. 19)***. Leave a 6" (15 cm) opening unpinned along one side.

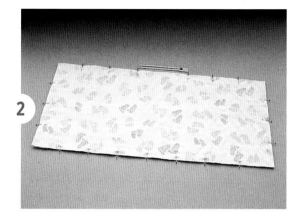

3 Set the machine for a straight stitch of 10 to 12 stitches per inch, or 2 to 2.5 mm. Place the pinned fabric under the presser foot just ahead of the opening. Align the cut edges to the ½" (1.3 cm) ***seam allowance guide (p. 19)*** on the bed of the machine. The bulk of the fabric will extend to the left of the machine. ***Backstitch (p. 19)*** to the opening; stop. Then, stitch forward, guiding the cut edges along the ½" (1.3 cm) seam allowance guide. ***Remove pins as you come to them (p. 19)***. Stop stitching ½" (1.3 cm) from the edge at the corner, leaving the needle down in the fabric. (Turn the handwheel until the needle is down.)

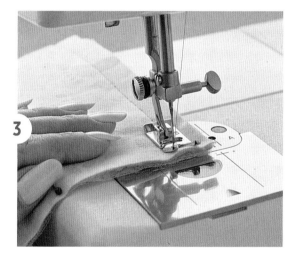

4 Raise the presser foot and turn the fabric a quarter turn. Lower the presser foot and continue stitching. Pivot in this manner at each corner. Stop stitching when you reach the last pin before the opening. Backstitch two or three stitches. ***Remove the fabric from the machine (p. 121)***.

TIP Mark a dot ½" (1.3 cm) from each corner on the wrong side of the lining. As you stitch toward each corner, you will be able to see exactly where you should stop.

5 *Trim the seam allowance corners diagonally (p. 96).* Press the seams flat to set the stitching line in the fabric. Insert a seam roll or wooden dowel into the opening and press the seam allowances open over the curved surface. In the area of the opening, turn back the seam allowances ½" (1.3 cm) and press.

6 Cut a 6" (15 cm) strip of paper-backed fusible web. Place the strip over the lining seam allowance at the opening, just inside the folded edge. Press over the strip to fuse it to the seam allowance, following the manufacturer's directions.

(continued)

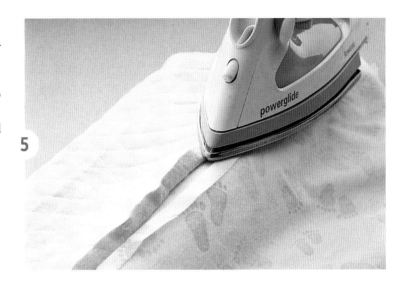

QUICK REFERENCE

Do not use the selvage. The tightly woven area along the outer edge of the fabric should be cut away in order to avoid puckering. Even if it looks flat, it will probably shrink and distort the sewn edge after laundering.

How to Sew a Nap-time Tote *continued*

7 Turn the pocket right side out through the opening. Insert a point turner or similar tool into the opening and gently push the pivot points out to form **perfect corners (p. 129)**. Remove the protective paper backing from the fusible web at the opening. Align the folded edges of the opening. Press over the opening from the lining side to fuse it closed. Press the remaining outer edges.

8 Mark the centers of two opposite sides of the tote piece; also mark the centers of the two short ends of the pocket. Center the pocket over the tote, right sides up. The pocket ends should be 2½" (6.5 cm) from the tote ends. Pin the pocket in place along both long edges, inserting pins perpendicular to the pocket edges.

9 Place the fabric under the presser foot so that the right edge of the foot is aligned to the side of the pocket and the back of the foot is aligned to the pocket end. Backstitch to the pocket end. Then, stitch forward to the opposite end; backstitch a few stitches. This is called topstitching. Repeat for the opposite side of the pocket.

TIP On most machines the right edge of the presser foot is ¼" (6 mm) from the needle tip. If this is not true of your machine, determine a different way to guide the stitching line ¼" (6 mm) from the pocket edge.

10 Mark two lines across the pocket, each 1" (2.5 cm) from the center. Stitch on the marked lines, backstitching at each end of each line. This will divide the pocket into two. Mark and stitch a line down the center of one pocket side, to divide it for carrying bottles.

11 Press a handle piece in half lengthwise. Open the fold and turn the long edges in, aligning them to the center crease; press. Refold the center, encasing the raw edges. Pin the layers together. Repeat for the other handle. Topstitch ¼" (6 mm) from both edges of each handle.

12 Pin the ends of one handle to the tote edge above one pocket, with the inner edges of the handle 3" (7.5 cm) from the center. Pin the other handle in the same position at the opposite edge. Stitch across the ends within the ½" (1.3 cm) seam allowance.

(continued)

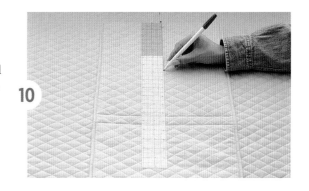

10

11

12

How to Sew a Nap-time Tote continued

13 Apply basting tape (page 34) to the right side of the zipper tape, running it along both outer edges. Remove the protective paper backing.

14 Place the closed zipper facedown along one of the sides that doesn't have a handle, aligning the edges. The ***zipper stops*** at the top and bottom of the zipper should be ½" (1.3 cm) from the ends of the tote. Attach the zipper foot to the sewing machine, and adjust the machine so that the ***needle will be stitching on the left side of the foot***. Set the machine for long straight stitches. Baste the zipper tape to the fabric, stitching ⅜" (1 cm) from the edge.

TIP Measure ⅜" (1 cm) from the outer edge of the zipper tape, and draw a guideline, using a pencil.

15 Adhere the other zipper tape edge to the opposite side of the tote as in step 14. Separate the zipper halves, and baste the other half in the same way. Pin the tote over the lining, right sides together, aligning all the edges and encasing the zipper and handles. Leave an opening between the handles on one end.

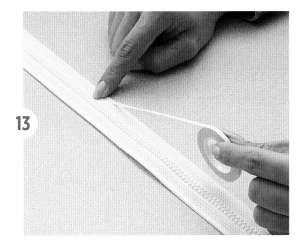

13

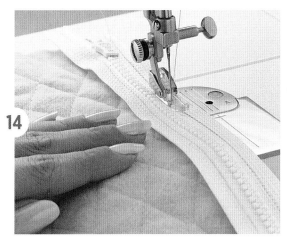

14

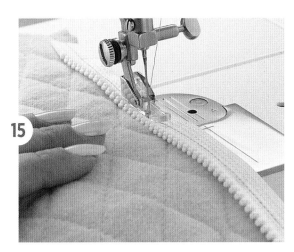

15

16 Place the fabric under the zipper foot, with the tote fabric on top, starting over one handle. Stitch ½" (1.3 cm) seam all around the tote, backstitching after and before the opening, and pivoting at the corners as in steps 2 and 3.

17 Trim the corners, press the seam allowances, turn the tote right side out, and close the opening as in steps 5 to 7 for the pocket. Attach the all-purpose presser foot. Topstitch ¼" (6 mm) from the edge all around the tote.

QUICK REFERENCE

Zipper stops. Tiny bars at the top of the zipper prevent the zipper slide from sliding right off the end. On a separating zipper, the larger stop at the bottom secures and aligns the zipper teeth.

Needle will be stitching on the left side of the foot. On some machines, the needle position is adjustable; on others, the foot position is adjustable. Check your owner's manual for the correct way to set your machine.

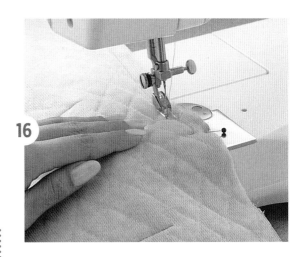

Round Tablecloth

A round table dressed with a floor-length tablecloth is an elegant accent in any room and also provides hidden storage space. This tablecloth features welting (page 35) at the outer edge which simplifies hemming and adds a designer touch. Single-fold bias tape (page 34) can also be used to sew a simple hem. Select fabric for the tablecloth that will drape in soft folds as it falls from the tabletop. To eliminate the need for matching a pattern at the seam, look for solid colors or small allover prints.

WHAT YOU'LL LEARN . . . .

- How to measure and determine the amount of fabric needed for a round tablecloth
- How to cut an accurate circle
- Two easy ways to finish a curved edge

WHAT YOU'LL NEED . . . .

- Fabric, amount determined in step 1
- Steel tape measure
- Fabric marking pen
- Thread
- Fabric-covered welting or single-fold bias tape to match or contrast with tablecloth fabric, amount equal to 3½ times the diameter of the tablecloth

TIP Most decorator fabrics are 48" or 54" (122 or 137 cm) wide. You will probably have to sew together at least one full width and one or two partial widths of fabric to obtain the necessary diameter. The length of each piece will equal the diameter of your tablecloth.

How to Sew a Round Tablecloth with a Welted Hem

1 Measure the tabletop diameter and the desired drop length for your tablecloth. Determine the amount of fabric needed, working with the following formula. (We used these numbers for our tablecloth on page 156; your numbers will probably be different.)

(continued)

Table diameter:	28" (71 cm)
Add the drop length twice	+ 29" (73.5 cm)
to find the diameter of the	+ 29" (73.5 cm)
tablecloth	= 86" (218.5 cm)
Divide by the fabric width	÷ 54" (137 cm)
Round up to the nearest whole	= 1.59
number to find the number	
of fabric widths needed	2
Multiply by the tablecloth	× 86" (218.5 cm)
diameter (above)	
to find the amount of fabric	= 172"(437 cm)
needed	
Convert to yards (meters);	4⅞ yd. (4.5 m)
round up	

How to Sew a Round Tablecloth with a Welted Hem continued

2 Prepare your fabric (page 41). Measure and mark the location of the cuts (equal to the tablecloth diameter) along the selvage. Cut the lengths following the cutting guidelines on pages 42 and 43. Trim away the selvages, cutting just beyond the tightly woven area.

3 Determine where you want the seam(s) in your tablecloth, using the diagrams as a guide. Cut one of the fabric widths as directed for either option A or B.

Option A

Use one seam when the diameter of the tablecloth is less than one-and-one-half times the fabric width. Subtract the fabric width from the tablecloth diameter. Cut a strip on the lengthwise grain of one fabric piece that is 2" (5 cm) wider than this measurement.

Option B

Use two seams when the diameter of the tablecloth is more than one-and-one half times the fabric width. **Cut one fabric piece in half lengthwise**.

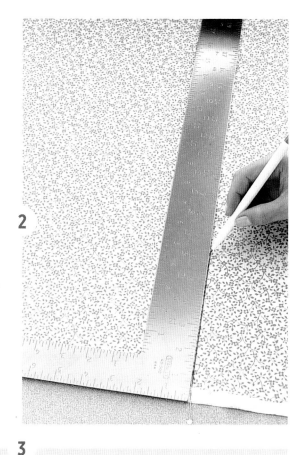

2

3

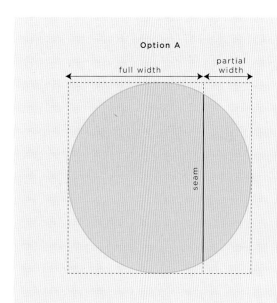

Option A

full width | partial width

seam

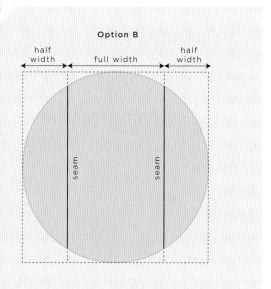

Option B

half width | full width | half width

seam | seam

4 Pin a partial- or a half-width piece to the full-width piece, right sides together, along the lengthwise edges, *inserting the pins perpendicular to the edges (p. 19)*. Place the pinned edges under the presser foot with the edges aligned to the ½" (1.3 cm) *seam allowance guide (p. 19)*. The bulk of the fabric is to the left of the machine.

5 Set the machine for a straight stitch with 10 to 12 stitches per inch, which equals 2 to 2.5 mm. Stitch a ½" (1.3 cm) seam, removing the pins as you come to them.

(continued)

QUICK REFERENCE

Cut one fabric piece in half lengthwise. Fold one width of fabric in half on the lengthwise grain. Press the fold and cut along the fold line.

How to Sew a Round Tablecloth with a Welted Hem *continued*

6 If you chose option B, stitch the second narrow piece to the opposite side of the full-width piece, following steps 4 and 5. Set the machine for a wide zigzag stitch with a length of 10 stitches per inch, which equals 2.5 mm. Stitch close to the edge of each seam allowance so that the right-hand stitches go just over the edge. This step, called a seam finish, keeps the edges from raveling.

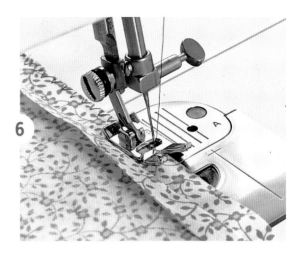

7 Press over the stitching line of the closed seams; then spread the layers apart, open the seam allowances, and press them again.

TIP Pressing the seam flat before pressing it open sets the stitches in the seamline and ultimately makes a better looking seam.

8 Fold the fabric in half lengthwise, then cross-wise, aligning the outer edges of the four layers. Pin the layers together to keep them from slipping. Using a steel tape measure and a fabric marking pen, mark an arc on the fabric, measuring the radius (one-half the diameter) of the tablecloth from the center folded corner of the fabric. Cut on the marked line through all four layers of fabric; remove the pins.

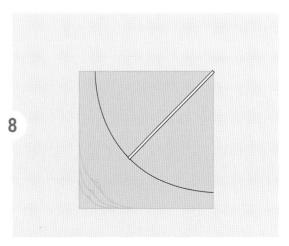

9 Pin the welting to the right side of the tablecloth along the outer edge, aligning the raw edges and **easing** the welting as you pin. Overlap, but don't cut, the ends.

10 Set the machine back to a straight stitch. Attach the zipper foot (page 11) and adjust it to the right of the needle. If your zipper foot is not adjustable, adjust the needle to the left of the foot. Slowly stitch the welting to the fabric, stitching over the existing stitches in the welting. Begin 2" (5 cm) from the end of the welting; remove pins as you come to them.

(continued)

(continued)

QUICK REFERENCE

Easing is a technique used when working with bias edges, such as the welting fabric. Avoid stretching the welting, keeping it relaxed as you pin or stitch it.

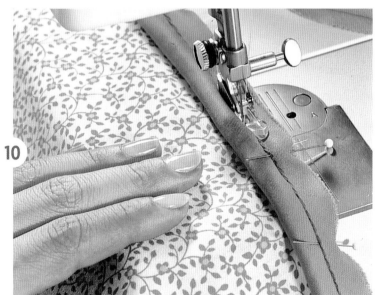

How to Sew a Round Tablecloth with a Welted Hem continued

11 Stop stitching 2" (5 cm) from the point where the ends of the welting will meet. Cut off the end of the welting so it overlaps the beginning end by 1" (2.5 cm). Remove the stitching from the overlapping end of the welting, exposing the inner cording; trim the end of the cording so it just meets the other end.

TIP If you are using packaged welting and need to splice pieces together, use the technique in steps 11 and 12 to make a continuous welting while you are sewing it to the edge.

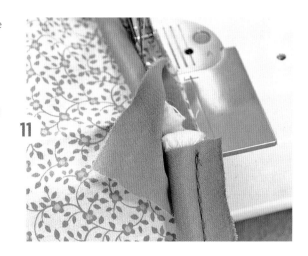

12 Fold under ½" (1.3 cm) of the fabric on the overlapping end of the welting. Wrap it around the beginning end and finish stitching it to the edge of the tablecloth.

13 Turn under the edges so the welting is at the outer edge of the tablecloth. Press lightly. Attach the general purpose presser foot, and reset the needle position to standard, if you changed it. With the right side up, stitch one more time around the outer edge, guiding the right edge of the presser foot along the welting edge and keeping the seam allowances turned under.

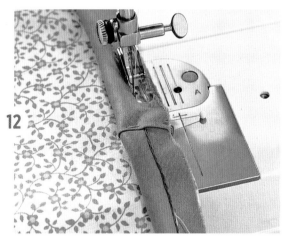

Alternate Hemming Method Using Bias Tape

1 Follow steps 1 to 8, adding ½" (1.3 cm) to the tablecloth diameter before cutting. Open one fold of the bias tape. Pin the tape to the right side of the tablecloth along the outer edge, keeping the raw edges even and easing the tape as you pin. Overlap the ends about ½" (1.3 cm).

2 Straight-stitch around the edge, stitching in the crease of the tape fold. Remove pins as you come to them. Overlap the stitches ½" (1.3 cm).

3 Turn the tape to the underside so the seam is exactly on the edge. Press. Secure the tape temporarily with fabric glue stick. Stitch as close as possible to the inner fold of the tape.

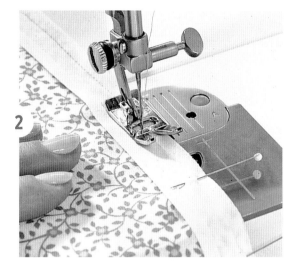

Rectangular Tablecloth

A simple rectangular tablecloth adds pattern or accents your color scheme and is easily changed for special holidays, the changing seasons, or your mood! The neatly mitered corners look very professional, yet they are surprisingly easy to sew. This technique can be used for several other home decorating items, such as a square table topper to place over a floor-length round tablecloth, dinner napkins, placemats, or a dresser scarf.

WHAT YOU'LL LEARN . . . .

- How to sew double-fold hems
- How a glue stick will help to make perfect mitered corners
- Even easy-to-sew items can make dramatic decorating statements

WHAT YOU'LL NEED . . . .

- Fabric, amount determined in step 1
- Thread
- Fabric glue stick

How to Sew a Rectangular Tablecloth

1 Determine the desired finished size for your tablecloth; add 4" (10 cm) to both length and width for the hem. Cut a rectangle of fabric equal to these measurements, following the cutting guidelines on pages 42 and 43.

TIP Select fabric that is wide enough for your tablecloth to be sewn in one piece: 48" (122 cm) fabric for a finished width up to 44" (112 cm), 54" (137 cm) fabric for a finished width up to 50" (127 cm), or 60" (152.5 cm) fabric for a finished width up to 56" (142 cm).

(continued)

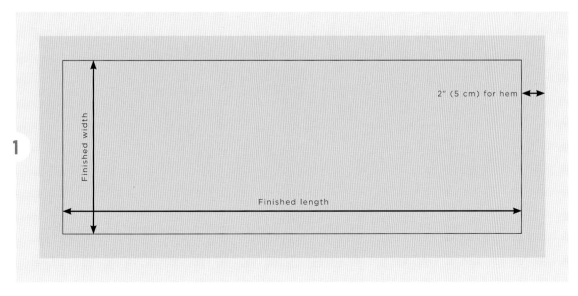

1

Finished width

2" (5 cm) for hem

Finished length

How to Sew a Rectangular Tablecloth continued

2 Press under 2" (5 cm) on all four edges of the cloth. Unfold the pressed edges and press each corner diagonally at the point where the creases intersect. Trim off the corner diagonally at the points where it crosses the foldlines. Use a dot of fabric glue stick to hold the corner in place.

3 Turn each cut edge in, aligning it to the first fold line, and press the outer fold.

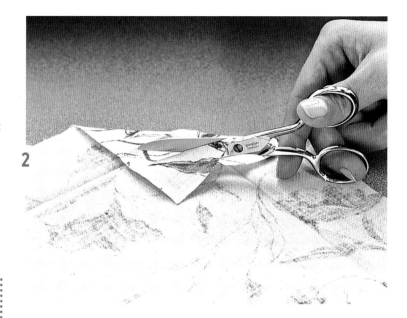

QUICK REFERENCE

Edgestitch. Stitch as close as possible to the inner edge of the hem. Align the presser foot so that the needle will enter the fabric just inside the inner edge. Note the point on the presser foot that aligns to the edge of the hem itself. As you sew, watch the fabric as it passes under that point on the foot rather than watching the needle. Stitch slowly for the best control.

4 Refold on the first fold line, encasing the raw edge to form a 1" (2.5 cm) double-fold hem. Pin the hem in place, *inserting pins perpendicular to the folds (p. 19)*. Use additional dots of glue stick to secure the mitered folds in the corners.

5 *Edgestitch* along the inner fold line. At the corners, stop with the needle down in the fabric and pivot. Overlap the stitches ½" (1.3 cm) where they meet. Press the tablecloth.

TIP Support the bulk of the fabric to your left with a card table or other surface, so the fabric feeds easily as you stitch. This will help you maintain a nice straight stitching line.

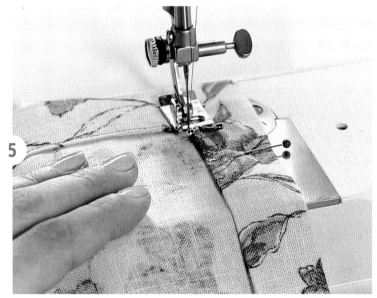

Lined Table Runner

Design and sew a nifty table runner to spark up your dining room table. Use a short runner as an accent in the center of the table or sew one that runs from end to end with an 8" to 10" (20.5 to 25.5 cm) drop length. For a table runner that is used as placemats, make it 18" (46 cm) wide. You can adjust both width and length to whatever size you might desire.

This runner is lined to the edge and can be made reversible by selecting two decorator fabrics. Welting (page 35), sewn into the outer edge of the runner, is available in many sizes and colors. For ease of application, choose welting no larger than ³⁄₁₆" (4.5 mm).

WHAT YOU'LL LEARN. . . . .

- How to insert narrow welting into the seam of a lined project
- Pointed ends are easy to create
- Your sewing skills are increasing

WHAT YOU'LL NEED . . . .

- Decorator fabric, amount depends on size of runner
- Lining fabric, same amount as decorator fabric
- Narrow welting, amount equal to slightly more than circumference of runner
- Thread

How to Sew a Lined Table Runner

1 Determine the desired finished length and width of your table runner. Add 1" (2.5 cm) to both measurements to allow for ½" (1.3 cm) seam allowances all around. Mark and cut a rectangle of decorator fabric for the front, following the cutting guidelines on pages 42 and 43. Cut the lining piece exactly the same size as the front.

TIP If you use the crosswise grain for the length, the maximum length of the runner is 1" (2.5 cm) shorter than the width of your fabric. Cutting the table runner on the lengthwise grain allows you to make it any length, but wastes more fabric. In that case, consider cutting both front and lining from the same fabric.

(continued)

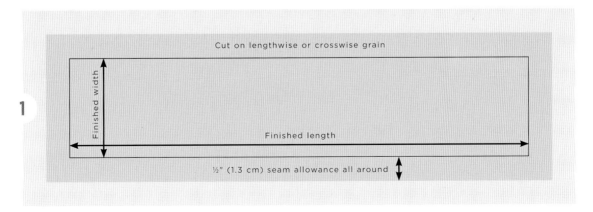

Cut on lengthwise or crosswise grain

Finished width

Finished length

½" (1.3 cm) seam allowance all around

1

How to Sew a Lined Table Runner continued

2 Fold the runner front in half lengthwise, aligning the cut edges; pin to keep the fabric from shifting. Mark a point 8½" (21.8 cm) from the end on the long cut edges. Draw a diagonal line from the mark on the side to the folded end. Carefully cut through both layers on the line, keeping the fabric edges aligned.

3 Repeat step 2 on the opposite end of the runner. Remove the pins and unfold the runner. Using the runner as a guide, cut points at the ends of the lining.

4 Pin the welting to the right side of the runner front along the outer edge, keeping the raw edges aligned and the welting relaxed. Plan for the ends to overlap along one long edge and leave tails unpinned. ***Insert the pins perpendicular to the edges (p. 19).***

TIP Keep the welting relaxed as you pin and actually "crowd" the welting slightly at the corners so that it will lie flat when it is turned to its final position.

5 Clip into the seam allowance of the welting at each corner of the runner at the exact point where the welting must bend. Clip **up to but not through** the stitching line, so that the welting seam allowances spread open and lie flat. Pin securely, keeping the raw edges of the welting and runner aligned.

6 Set the machine for a straight stitch of 10 stitches per inch, which equals 2.5 mm. Attach the zipper foot (page 11) and adjust it to the right of the needle. If your foot is not adjustable, adjust the needle to the left of the foot. Place the fabric under the presser foot 2" (5 cm) from the end of the welting. Slowly stitch the welting to the fabric, stitching over the existing stitches in the welting. **Remove pins as you come to them (p. 19)**.

(continued)

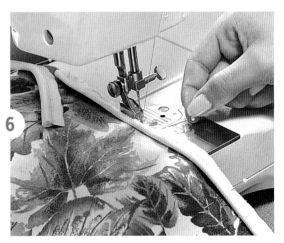

QUICK REFERENCE

Up to but not through means exactly what it says. Any time you clip into a seam allowance, the clip should be right up to the stitching, but it must not cut the stitching threads, or you will create a hole in the seam.

How to Sew a Lined Table Runner continued

7 When you reach a corner, stop with the needle down in the fabric at the point of the clip. Lift the presser foot and pivot the fabric so the stitching line of the welting on the next side is in line with the needle. Lower the presser foot and continue stitching around the runner, pivoting at each corner.

8 Stop stitching 2" (5 cm) from the point where the ends of the welting will meet. Cut off the end of the welting so it overlaps the beginning end by 1" (2.5 cm). Remove the stitching from the overlapping end of the welting, exposing the inner cording; trim the end of the cording so it just meets the other end.

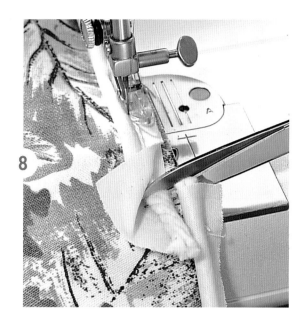

9 Fold under ½" (1.3 cm) of the fabric on the overlapping end of the welting. Wrap it around the beginning and finish stitching it to the runner, overlapping the stitches ½" (1.3 cm) where they meet.

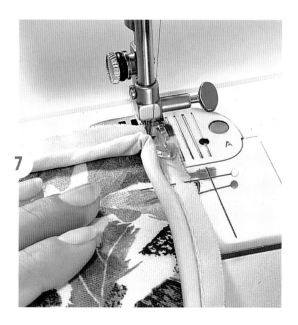

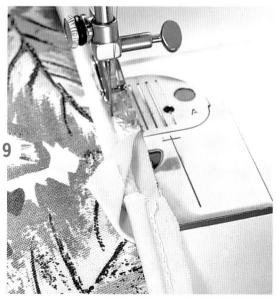

10 Press along the stitching line with the tip of your iron to relax the fabric and set the seam. Check that the fabric does not ripple or draw up where you have attached the welting.

11 Pin the front over the lining, right sides together, encasing the welting between the layers and aligning the outer edges. Leave a 7" (18 cm) opening unpinned along one side. Place the table runner under the presser foot, lining side down, just ahead of the unpinned area. Remove the pin marking the end of the opening before lowering the presser foot.

(continued)

How to Sew a Lined Table Runner continued

12 *Backstitch (p. 19)* three or four stitches; then stitch forward **over the previous stitches**, actually "crowding" the welting as you stitch. Pivot at each corner, and stop stitching at the opposite side of the opening. Backstitch three or four stitches, and **remove the fabric from the machine (p. 121)**.

13 *Trim the seam allowances diagonally (p. 96)* at each corner. Turn back and press the lining seam allowance ½" (1.3 cm) from the edge in the unstitched area.

QUICK REFERENCE

Over the previous stitches. The second stitching line must be exactly over the first stitching line or slightly closer to the welting, so that the first stitching line does not show after the runner is turned right side out.

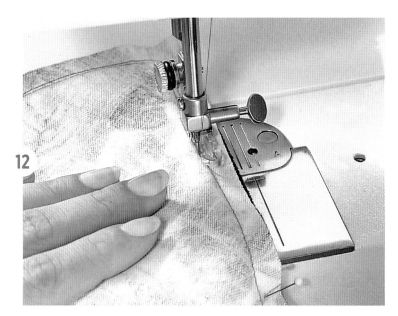

14 Reach in through the unstitched opening to grasp an end of the runner and pull it through the opening. Repeat for the other end, turning the runner right side out.

15 Use a point turner (page 33) to push out the corners, if necessary. Press the table runner up to the welting as you smooth and tug the welting out to the edge with your fingers. Slipstitch the opening closed, following the directions on page 22.

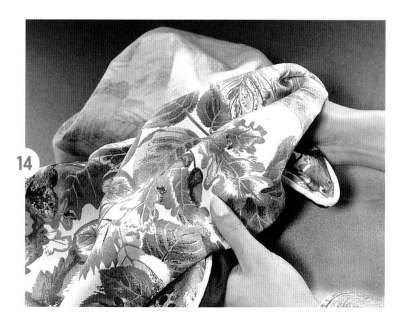

Quilted Placemats

Reversible machine-quilted placemats add style to your dining room and, because they are easy to sew, help you gain confidence in your sewing skills. Placemats can be made in any size and shape. These rectangular placemats are a common finished size of 12" × 18" (30.5 × 46 cm).

Choose firmly woven, lightweight to mediumweight fabrics. Look for coordinating prints or solid color fabrics for the front and back, and purchase extra fabric to make matching napkins. Low-loft polyester or poly/cotton blend batting (page 35) is a good choice for placemats. It provides a subtle quilted look and holds up well through frequent laundering. The fabric and batting amounts suggested are enough for four placemats.

WHAT YOU'LL LEARN . . . .

- How to line a project to the edge
- How to use batting
- Quilting by machine is really very simple

WHAT YOU'LL NEED . . . .

- ¾ yd. (0.7 m) fabric for placemat fronts
- ¾ yd. (0.7 m) fabric for placemat backs
- ¾ yd. (0.7 m) low-loft batting
- Thread to match
- Erasable marking pen or chalk (page 28)
- 6" × 24" (15 × 61 cm) quilter's ruler or yardstick (meterstick)
- Walking foot (page 11), optional

How to Sew a Quilted Placemat

1 Preshrink your fabric (page 33). Cut one 13" × 19" (33 × 48.5 cm) rectangle of fabric for each placemat front and one 13" × 19" (33 × 48.5 cm) rectangle of fabric for each placemat back, following the cutting guidelines on pages 42 and 43. Remember to align the edges to the lengthwise and crosswise grainlines. Also cut one 13" × 19" (33 × 48.5 cm) rectangle of batting for each placemat.

(continued)

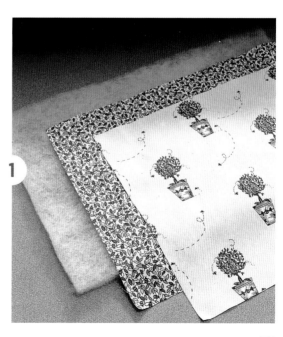

How to Sew a Quilted Placemat continued

2 Mark a point 2½" (6.5 cm) from one side on the placemat front, near the upper edge, with chalk or an air soluble pen. Make additional marks across the top every 2" (5 cm). The last mark should be 2½" (6.5 cm) from the opposite side. Repeat the marks along the lower edge. Draw parallel lines across the placemat front, connecting the marks. These are your **quilting lines**. Mark small dots ½" (1.3 cm) from the edges in each corner, on the wrong side of the placemat back.

3 Place the placemat front, right side up, on top of the batting, aligning the cut edges. Place the placemat back over the front, right sides together and align all four edges. Pin the layers together, along the outer edges, **inserting the pins perpendicular to the edges (p. 19)**. In the center of one end, leave a 6" (15 cm) opening unpinned.

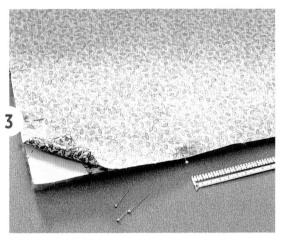

4 Set the machine for a straight stitch of 10 stitches per inch, which equals 2.5 mm. Place the fabrics under the presser foot, with the batting against the bed of the machine. Align the needle to enter the fabric just ahead of the opening with the cut edges of the fabrics aligned to the ½" (1.3 cm) **seam allowance guide (p. 19)** on the throat plate of your machine. Remove the pin that marks the opening before lowering the presser foot.

> **QUICK REFERENCE**
>
> **Quilting lines.** It is easier to mark these lines when the fabric is flat, before adding the batting and lining. Use a marker that can be easily removed; test to be sure. You'll find several markers to choose from in the notions department. Use air-soluble marker only if you are confident you will finish the project in one sewing session.

5 *Backstitch (p. 19)* three or four stitches; then stitch forward until you come to the dot in the first corner. Stop the machine with the needle completely down in the fabric at the dot.

6 Lift the presser foot and turn the fabric so the next side aligns to the ½" (1.3 cm) seam allowance guide. Lower the presser foot and continue stitching around all four sides, pivoting in this manner at each corner. Stop stitching at the opposite side of the opening; backstitch three or four stitches.

(continued)

How to Sew a Quilted Placemat continued

7 *Remove the fabric from the machine (p. 121)* and trim the threads close to the fabric. Press the outer edges flat to set the stitches in the seam. Trim the batting seam allowance close to the stitching line and trim the batting away ½" (1.3 cm) from the edge in the opening area. **Trim the seam allowances diagonally (p. 96)** at each corner, cutting ⅛" (3 mm) from the stitches.

8 *Turn back the back seam allowance* and press, applying light pressure with the tip of the iron down the crease of the seam. In the area of the opening, turn back and press the seam allowance ½" (1.3 cm).

9 Turn the placemat over; turn back and press the remaining seam allowance of the opening. Turn the placemat right side out, reaching in through the opening to pull out each corner. Insert a point turner or similar tool into the placemat, gently pushing the points out to form **perfect corners (p. 129)**.

7

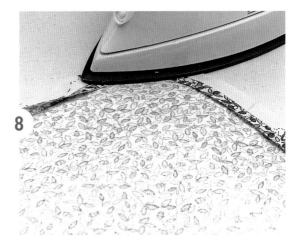

8

9

10 Press the placemat flat, keeping the seam right on the edge of the placemat. Pin the opening closed, aligning the folded edges and placing the pins perpendicular to the edge. *Edgestitch (p. 169)* around the placemat, stitching the opening closed; pivot at each corner. Overlap the stitches where they meet.

11 *Pin-baste* the layers together with small safety pins, working from the center to the sides. Place the pins about 4" (10 cm) apart and half-way between the marked lines so they won't get in the way of the presser foot while you are stitching on the quilting lines.

12 Attach a walking foot (page 11), if you have one, or use a general-purpose foot. Place the fabric under the presser foot, aligning the needle to the beginning of a marked quilting line near the center of the placemat. Lower the foot. Turn the handwheel by hand for one stitch, and stop with the needle at the highest position. Raise the foot and pull on the needle thread to bring the bobbin thread up through the fabric.

(continued)

QUICK REFERENCE

Turn back the back seam allowance. It is difficult to fit a seam roll or hard cardboard tube into a placemat to press the seam allowances open. Turning back and pressing one seam allowance helps to separate them and make the seam look neater from the outside.

Pin-baste. Traditionally quilting projects are basted with a needle and thread, which, though more time-consuming, is certainly an alternative here. The basting is necessary to keep the fabrics and batting from shifting around while you quilt. Quilters often use safety pins that are angled for easier insertion. Pin-basting is a convenient method as long as you don't have to stop and remove the safety pins as you go along.

How to Sew a Quilted Placemat *continued*

13 Set your stitch length at almost 0. Draw both threads under the presser foot to one side. Lower the foot, with the needle aligned to enter the fabric at the edge of the placemat. Stitch several very short stitches to secure the threads at the beginning of the stitching line.

14 Increase the stitch length to 10 stitches per inch, which equals 2.5 mm. Stitch forward on the quilting line across the placemat. Slow your stitching as you approach the opposite side. Just before you reach the edge, decrease the stitch length to almost 0. Take several stitches to secure the threads. Remove the fabric from the machine.

TIP Keep both hands on the fabric as shown to ensure smooth, even stitching. However, don't pull or push; let the walking foot move the fabric. If you don't have a walking foot, it may be helpful to "flatten" the fabric in front of the foot with your fingers

15 Follow steps 12 to 14 to machine-quilt on each marked line, working from the center out to the sides. Stitch in the same direction on each line to prevent diagonal ripples from forming between the quilting lines. When all the quilting is done, trim all the threads close to the fabric. Remove the safety pins.

TIP Steam the placemat lightly to "puff up" the quilting. Do not touch the iron to the fabric as you steam.

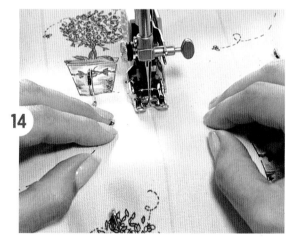

How to Sew Super Easy Napkins

1 Cut off the selvages from the fabric. Cut out square napkins, following the grainlines exactly. Pull threads out of the crosswise and lengthwise grains to mark the cutting lines, if possible (page 43). For the most efficient use of your fabric, divide the full width of 45", 48", or 54" (115, 122, or 137 cm) fabric into three equal squares. If your fabric is 60" (152.5 cm) wide, cut either four 15" (38 cm) or three 20" (51 cm) napkins.

2 Set your machine for a narrow zigzag stitch, about 12 stitches per inch, which equals 2 mm. Stitch ½" (1.3 cm) from he edge around each napkin, pivoting ½" (1.3 cm) from the corners.

3 Pull threads to fray the outer edges on each side of the napkin, working from the cut edges up to the stitching.

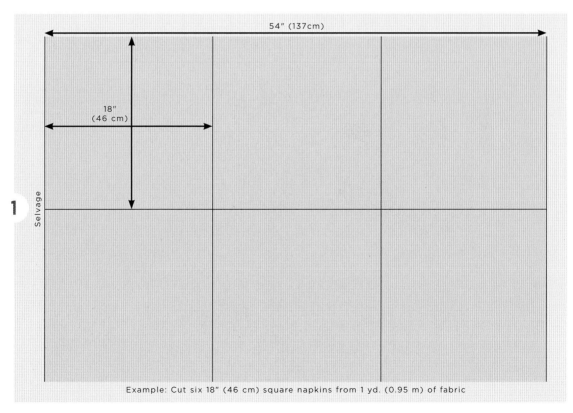

Example: Cut six 18" (46 cm) square napkins from 1 yd. (0.95 m) of fabric

More Table Runners and Placemats

Sew placemats from checked fabric and quilt them, following the lines of the check. Sew matching napkins, following the general directions for a rectangular tablecloth (page 165), but using ½" (6 mm) double-fold hems.

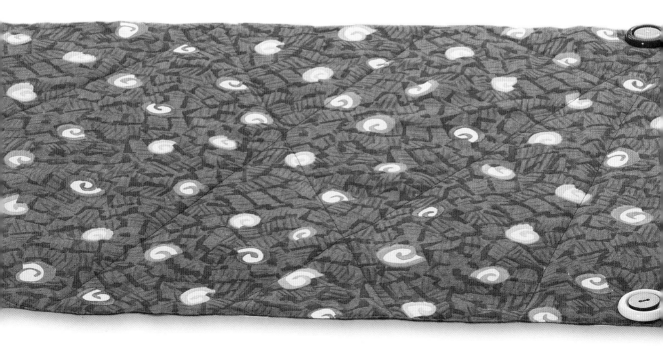

Use a dinner plate to round off the corners of a rectangle, creating an oval table runner or placemats. Omit batting in the placemats and add welting to the outer seam. Remember to ease (not stretch) the welting around the curves.

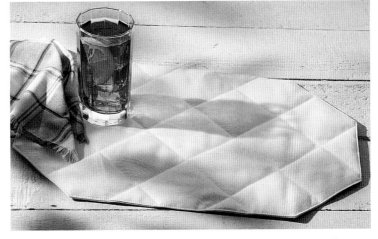

Make octagonal placemats. Prepare a paper pattern; cut off the corners diagonally, 3½" (9 cm) from the corners. Plan your quilting lines to echo the shape of the placemat.

Omit the welting; add batting between the layers of a table runner, and quilt it in random diagonal lines. Sew colorful buttons along the angled ends of the table runner.

Roman Shade

A Roman shade is a tailored, economical window treatment that controls light and provides privacy. This version is lined to provide added body, prevent fabric fading, and create a uniform appearance from the outside. Mounted on a board, the shade can be installed as an inside mount (as shown here), securing it inside the upper window frame, flush with the front of the frame. For an outside mount, the shade is installed on the wall at least 1" (2.5 cm) above the frame. Choose a sturdy, firm decorator fabric to give the shade a crisp look. These directions are suitable for a shade that is at least 2" (5 cm) narrower than the fabric width.

WHAT YOU'LL LEARN

- The importance of accurate measuring and cutting
- How to cover and install a mounting board
- A simple way to line a window treatment
- How to use fusible web
- How a Roman shade actually works

WHAT YOU'LL NEED

- Decorator fabric, amount determined in step 4
- Drapery lining fabric, amount equal to shade fabric
- Thread to match
- Mounting board, 1 × 2 nominal lumber
- White glue
- 1" (2.5 cm) angle irons, for outside mount
- ¾" (2 cm) paper-backed fusible web (page 34)
- Graph paper
- Screw eyes
- Plastic rings, ⅜" or ½" (1 or 1.3 cm)
- Shade cord
- Flat metal weight bar, ½" (1.3 cm) wide, cut ½" (1.3 cm) shorter than finished width of shade
- Awning cleat
- Staple gun and staples
- Drapery pull (optional)

How to Sew a Roman Shade

TIP Nominal lumber, angle irons, screw eyes, flat metal bars, awning cleats, and drapery pulls can all be purchased at a hardware store. If you do not have the proper tools, ask them to cut the lumber and metal bar to the size you need.

1 Measure the width of the window frame. Cut a 1 × 2 board 2" (5 cm) longer than the outside measurement, for an outside mount or ½" (1.3 cm) shorter than the inside measurement, for an inside mount. Cut a strip of fabric for covering the board ½" (1.3 cm) wider than the board circumference and 2" (5 cm) longer than the board length. Center the board on the strip; wrap the fabric over the ends, and secure with glue. Then wrap the length of the board, overlapping the fabric down the center of one side and folding out excess fabric neatly at the ends; secure with glue. Allow to dry. Disregard steps 2 and 3 if you are installing an inside mount.

2 Place the 1" (2.5 cm) angle irons on the side of the board opposite the overlap, about 2" (5 cm) from each end of the board. Mark the screw holes and, using a drill and appropriate drill bit, predrill holes into the board for the screws. Screw the angle irons to the board.

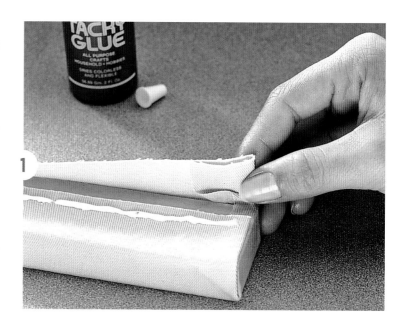

3 Hold the board above the window, making sure it is level and centered over the window frame; mark the screw holes on the wall. Secure the angle irons to the wall, using 1½" (3.8 cm) flat-head screws. If the angle irons are not at wall studs, use molly bolts or plastic anchors.

4 Determine the finished length of the shade. For an outside mount, measure from the top of the mounting board to the sill or ½" (1.3 cm) below the apron; for an inside mount, measure the inside frame to the sill. The finished width of the shade is equal to the length of the mounting board *plus ¼" (6 mm)*.

(continued)

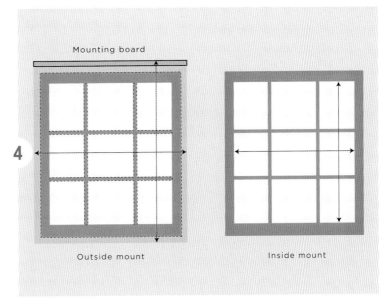

Mounting board

Outside mount

Inside mount

QUICK REFERENCE

Plus ¼" (6 mm). By sewing the shade slightly wider than the mounting board, you are sure to cover the entire board. There is always a little width and length lost in pressing and stitching the fabric.

How to Sew a Roman Shade continued

5 Calculate the cut length and cut width of the fabric, working with this formula. (We used these numbers for our Roman shade on page 186; your numbers will probably be different.) Cut the shade fabric; do not use a selvage as an edge. Cut the lining fabric with the width equal to the finished width and the length equal to the finished length plus 3½" (9 cm). Follow the guidelines for cutting decorator fabric on pages 42 and 43.

6 Press under 1" (2.5 cm) on the sides of the shade. Cut strips of ¾" (2 cm) paper-backed fusible web the length of each side. Turn back the hem and place the strips near the cut edge. Press over the strips to fuse them to the hem allowance, following the manufacturer's directions.

TIP Use a press cloth (page 31) to prevent any fusible adhesive from messing up the sole plate of your iron.

7 Place the lining over the shade fabric, wrong sides together, with the lower edge of the lining 3¾" (9 cm) above the lower edge of the shade fabric; tuck the lining under the side hems. Remove the protective paper backing from the fusible web, and press to fuse the hems in place.

5

Finished width:	45" (115 cm)
Add 2" (5 cm) for side hems	+ 2" (5 cm)
to find the cut width	= 47" (120 cm)

Finished length:	50" (127 cm)
Add 7" (18 cm) for hem	+ 7" (18 cm)
and mounting to find	= 57" (144.5 cm)
the cut length	

6

7

8 Press under ½" (1.3 cm) at the lower edge; then press under 3" (7.5 cm) to form the hem. (The second fold should be even with the lower edge of the lining.) Pin the hem, placing pins perpendicular to the hem.

9 *Edgestitch (p. 167)* along the inner fold-line of the hem, *backstitching (p. 19)* at the beginning and end, and *removing the pins as you come to them (p. 19)*. Press the entire shade lightly.

10 On the lining side, draw a line across the top of the shade at the finished length. Draw a second line 1½" (3.8 cm) above it for the *mounting board projection*. Cut off excess fabric along the top line. Pin the layers together, and finish the upper edges together using a wide zigzag stitch (page 21).

(continued)

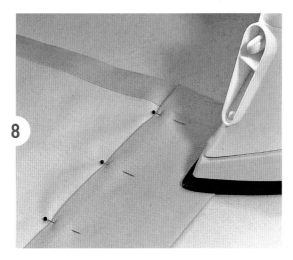

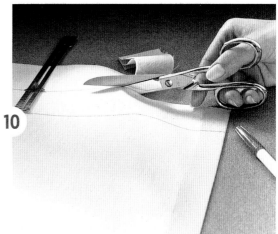

QUICK REFERENCE

Mounting board projection. The actual width of 1 × 2 nominal lumber is 1½" (3.8 cm) which is how far the front of the mounting board (and the shade) will stand away from the wall on an outside mount.

How to Sew a Roman Shade continued

11 Diagram on graph paper the back side of the shade, indicating the finished length and width. Mark the hem 3" (7.5 cm) from the lower edge. Plan the **locations of rings** in columns spaced 8" to 12" apart (20.5 to 30.5 cm), with the outer columns ¾" (2 cm) from the outer edges of the shade. Space them in even horizontal rows 5" to 8" (12.5 to 20.5 cm) apart with the bottom row at the top of the hem and the top row on the line marked in step 10. Work through the following formula to determine ring locations. (We used these numbers for our shade on page 186; your numbers will probably be different.)

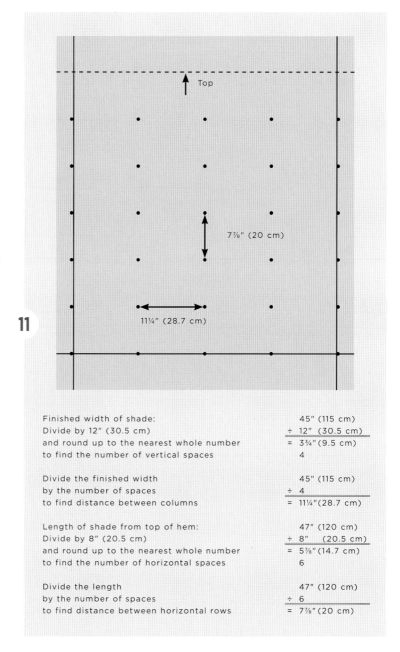

Finished width of shade:	45" (115 cm)
Divide by 12" (30.5 cm)	÷ 12" (30.5 cm)
and round up to the nearest whole number	= 3¾" (9.5 cm)
to find the number of vertical spaces	4

Divide the finished width	45" (115 cm)
by the number of spaces	÷ 4
to find distance between columns	= 11¼" (28.7 cm)

Length of shade from top of hem:	47" (120 cm)
Divide by 8" (20.5 cm)	÷ 8" (20.5 cm)
and round up to the nearest whole number	= 5⅞" (14.7 cm)
to find the number of horizontal spaces	6

Divide the length	47" (120 cm)
by the number of spaces	÷ 6
to find distance between horizontal rows	= 7⅞" (20 cm)

12 Mark the locations for the rings on the lining side of the shade, according to your diagram. The bottom row of rings is at the upper edge of the hem; the top row is the determined distance below the top marked line. (There are no rings on the top line.) Pin horizontally through both layers of fabric at each mark.

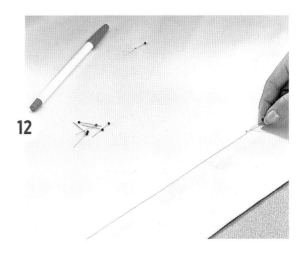

13 Thread a needle with a double strand of thread. Secure each ring with 4 or 5 small stitches, through both fabric layers. Reinforce all the rings in the bottom row with extra stitches because they carry the weight of the shade.

14 Insert the flat weight bar into the **hem pocket**; slipstitch (page 22) the end openings closed.

(continued)

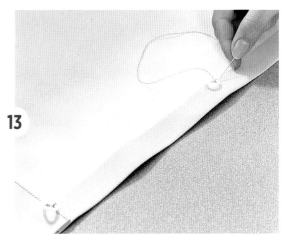

QUICK REFERENCE

Locations of rings. A system of evenly spaced rings through which cords are run on the back of the shade make it possible to raise and lower the shade. When the rings are spaced in even columns and rows, the shade will fold neatly at regular intervals when raised.

Hem pocket. In forming the hem at the lower edge, 3" (7.5 cm) openings were left on the sides so that the hem is really a tube or "pocket" into which you will slide the weight bar.

How to Sew a Roman Shade *continued*

15 Remove the mounting board from the angle irons, if you are installing an outside mount. Staple the shade to the top of the mounting board, aligning the marked line to the top front edge of the board.

16 Predrill the holes and insert screw eyes, centered, on the underside of the mounting board, aligning them to the columns of rings.

17 On the side where you want the cords to hang, run cord through the first column of rings, through the top screw eye, and **partway down the side**. Cut the cord and tie a nonslip knot at the bottom ring. Repeat for each column in order, running the cords also through the previous screw eyes. Apply glue to the knots for security.

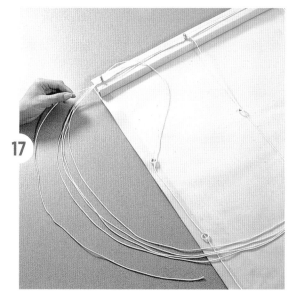

18 Reattach the mounting board to the angle irons for an outside mount or install the mounting board directly to the underside of the window frame, inserting screws through predrilled holes, for an inside mount. Adjust the cords with the shade down so the tension on all cords is equal. Tie the cords in a knot just below the first screw eye. Braid the cords, insert them through a drapery pull, if desired, and knot and trim the ends.

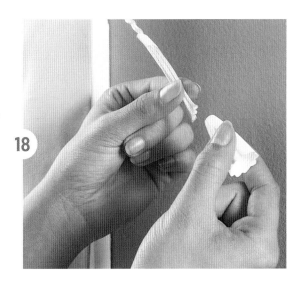

19 Secure an awning cleat to the edge of the window frame or on the wall. Pull gently on the cords to raise the shade, *forming soft folds*. Wind the cord around the cleat to hold the shade in its raised position.

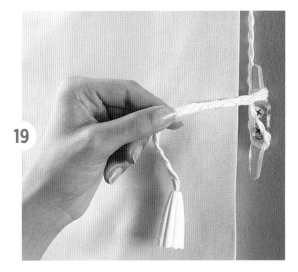

QUICK REFERENCE

Partway down the side. Work on one column at a time, cutting the cord only after you have run the cord through the appropriate rings and screw eyes and determined the extra length needed for raising and lowering the shade. The extra length needed may depend on the location of the window and whether or not you want it to be accessible to children.

Forming soft folds. The first time you raise the shade, you may have to "train" it where to fold. As you raise the shade, pull the excess fabric between horizontal rows forward, forming gentle rolls. To help it "remember," leave the shade in the raised position for a day or two.

Draped Lace Swags

Very little sewing is required to achieve this elegant decorator look. The key is in the selection of the fabric. Many laces, ranging in width from 48" to 60" (122 to 152.5 cm), have decorative selvages. From a short distance, most lace fabrics appear to be reversible, and, in some cases, you can use this fact to your advantage. In general, the right side of the lace has more texture, perhaps some raised, embroidered areas. The wrong side looks flat and less interesting. If you are unsure about which side is the right side, ask for clarification at the fabric store, and mark the right side.

You will use the entire width of the lace for the swag, running the lengthwise grain up one side, draping across the rod, and down the opposite side. Because the selvages are already finished, you merely sew narrow hems in the two cut ends of the lace. The effect is created in the way the lace is draped over the rod.

WHAT YOU'LL LEARN . . . .

- How to measure the window for a swag
- How to sew double-fold hems (p. 98)
- Making decorator window treatments is easier than you thought!

WHAT YOU'LL NEED . . . .

- Lace fabric in the amount determined in step 1
- Thread to match the fabric
- Decorative curtain rod of your choice, in a length suitable for the window width
- Tools and hardware, for installing the rod

How to Sew a Draped Lace Swag

1 Mount the rod above the window frame, with the outer brackets just clearing the frame sides. To determine the fabric length needed, drape a cord in the path you want the lower edge of the swag to follow. Cut the lace swag panel to this length, following the cutting directions on page 42.

(continued)

How to Sew a Draped Lace Swag continued

2 ***Press under*** 1" (2.5 cm) on one end of the swag panel.

3 Unfold the pressed edge. Turn the cut edge back, aligning it to the first foldline; press the outer fold.

QUICK REFERENCE

Press under. Place the fabric face-down on your ironing board. Fold the cut edge back; measure, and press, keeping the width of the folded edge consistent across the entire edge.

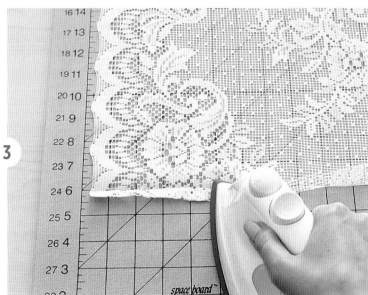

4 Refold the edge along the pressed foldlines, encasing the raw edge to form a ½" (1.3 cm) double-fold hem. Pin the hem, **inserting the pins perpendicular to the folds (p. 19)**.

5 Place the pinned hem under the presser foot of the machine, with the wrong side of the panel facing up. The bulk of the fabric is positioned to the left of the machine. The selvage of the panel should be even with the back of the presser foot, with the needle aligned to enter the fabric just inside the inner fold.

(continued)

How to Sew a Draped Lace Swag continued

6 **Backstitch (p. 19)** along the inner fold to the selvage. Reverse the direction and stitch forward, stitching the entire length of the hem to the opposite selvage. **Remove pins as you come to them (p. 19)**. Stop stitching at the opposite selvage. Backstitch for about ½" (1.3 cm).

7 Lift the presser foot, and **remove the fabric from the machine (p. 121)**.

8 Drape the swag panel over the rod, as shown in the photograph on page 196, placing the hemmed end in the desired location. Mark the unstitched end at the desired location for the opposite hem.

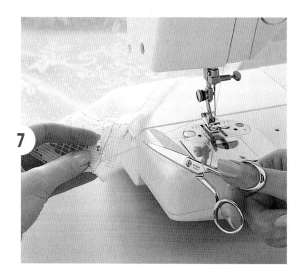

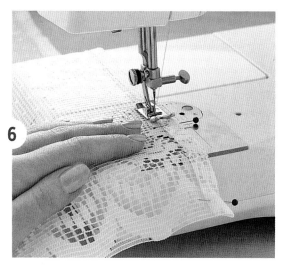

9 Remove the swag panel from the rod. Cut the panel 1" (2.5 cm) longer than the mark, allowing for the double hem. Stitch the remaining hem, following steps 2 to 7.

10 Fanfold the entire finished panel into gentle pleats of consistent depth. Tie the folded fabric at regular intervals, using ribbon or twill tape. Drape the folded panel over the rod, and arrange the folds as shown in the photograph on page 196.

Rod-pocket Treatments

Many window fashions are hung from a pole or rod by means of a "pocket" sewn along the upper edge. Thus the name, "rod-pocket" treatments. Styles vary depending on the rod or pole used, the depth of the heading, the length of the curtain or top treatment, the fullness of the style, and the way the style is arranged once it has been mounted over the window. There are also added embellishments, such as decorative trims or tie-backs, that can give the treatment a distinctive look.

For now, though, let's just focus on a basic rod-pocket valance and identify its parts. The diagram below shows that the valance is really a flat rectangle of fabric. The sides and bottom of the rectangle are hemmed with **double-fold hems (p. 98)**. The top is folded to the back and sewn with two stitching lines. The heading, from the top fold to the top stitching line, forms a ruffle above the rod when the valance is mounted. The area between the stitching lines is the rod pocket. Designed to have two times fullness, the rectangle is made twice as wide as the desired finished width of the valance. Note that this valance required two widths of fabric. One is centered and the other is cut in half and sewn to each side, thus avoiding a distracting center seam.

WHAT YOU'LL LEARN. . . . .

- How to determine the amount of fabric needed for any rod-pocket treatment
- Basic steps for sewing any rod-pocket treatment
- There are lots of rod-pocket styles to choose from

WHAT YOU'LL NEED. . . . .

- Fabric, amount determined by working through the chart in step 1
- Thread to match fabric
- Curtain rod or pole
- Drapery weights (page 215) if sewing curtains

How to Sew a Rod-pocket Treatment

To determine the rod-pocket depth (A), measure around the widest part of the rod or pole. In some cases this may mean measuring in the crook of an elbow. Add ½" (1.3 cm) ease to this measurement, and divide the result by 2. This measurement will be the distance between stitching lines.

The height of the heading (B) can be adjusted to suit your taste, from very short at ½" (1.3 cm) to quite high at 4" (10 cm). Sometimes the heading is made extremely long so that it falls forward over the rod pocket, forming an attached valance (page 211) along the top of a rod-pocket curtain.

1 Measure the window and calculate the length of fabric needed for your valance or curtain, working with the formula, opposite: (We used these numbers for our valance on page 202; your numbers will probably be different.)

1

Finished length, measured from the bottom of the rod to the bottom of the treatment:		12"	(30.5 cm)
Add the total hem depth	+	4"	(10 cm)
Add the rod pocket depth twice	+	1¾"	(4.5 cm)
	+	1¾"	(4.5 cm)
Add the heading height twice	+	2½"	(6.5 cm)
	+	2½"	(6.5 cm)
Add ½" (1.3 cm) to turn under bottom of rod pocket	+	½"	(1.3 cm)
Add ½" (1.3 cm) for ease	+	½"	(1.3 cm)
to find the cut length of each piece	=	*25½"	(64.8 cm)
Multiply the window width		36"	(91.5 cm)
by the desired fullness	×	2½	
to find the finished width	=	90"	(229 cm)
Add the total side hem depth twice	+	2"	(5 cm)
	+	2"	(5 cm)
To find the total cut width needed	=	94"	(239 cm)
Divide the total cut width by the fabric width	÷	54"	(137 cm)
Round the number up to the nearest whole number	=	1.74	
to find the number of fabric widths needed		2	
Multiply this number by the cut length	×	25½"	(64.8 cm)
to find the length to buy	=	51"	(129.5 cm)

Because fabric stores sell fabric in whole yards (meters) or eighths of a yard (fractions of a meter), purchase the next largest amount. If you buy a fabric with a pattern repeat, follow the chart until you have determined the cut length*. Your actual cut length must be rounded up to the next number evenly divisible by the pattern repeat. For instance, if the pattern repeat is 15" (38 cm), your cut length will be 30" (76 cm), not 25½" (64.8 cm), because 30 (76) can be evenly divided by 15 (38). Proceed with the chart using this revised cut length measurement.

2 Preshrink your fabric (page 41). Measure and mark the location of each cut along the selvage. Cut the pieces, following the cutting guidelines on page 42. If you do not have to match a pattern (page 44), cut away the selvages, cutting just beyond the tightly woven area.

3 Pin two pieces together along the vertical edges, *inserting the pins perpendicular to the edges (p. 19)*. Match the pattern, if necessary, following the guidelines on page 44. Stitch ½" (1.3 cm) seam, *backstitching (p. 19)* at the beginning and end of the seam for about ½" (1.3 cm). *Remove pins as you come to them (p. 19)*.

(continued)

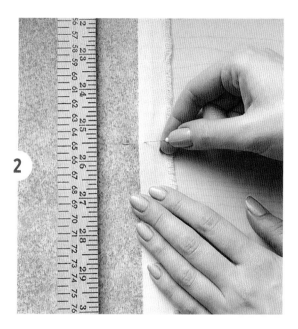

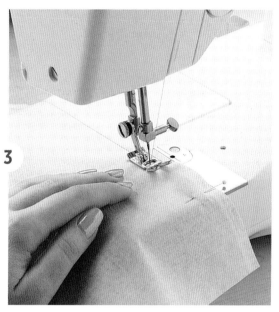

QUICK REFERENCE

Finished length. Valances are not only decorative, they also "cap" the window visually and hide mechanical workings of any undertreatments. As a general proportion guideline, the valance length is about one-fifth of the total distance from the top of the window to the floor. You can make your valance longer or shorter, if you prefer. Sketch the total window treatment to scale to help you make this decision.

Measure from the bottom of the rod. If you have not yet installed the rod, or even selected a rod, plan to install it so that the bottom of the rod is even with the top of the window frame. Then you can measure from the top of the frame to where you want the bottom edge of the valance or curtain to be.

Round up to the nearest whole number. Most window treatments that have some amount of fullness in them, including rod-pocket treatments, are sewn using full and half widths of fabric. Even if your treatment requires two-and-one-half widths of fabric, you have to purchase three full widths, and your yardage requirements have to be determined by rounding up to the nearest whole number.

How to Sew a Rod-pocket Treatment *continued*

4 Finish the raw edges together, using a zigzag stitch (page 21) set at medium width and medium length. Stitch so the right-hand swing of the needle just clears the fabric edge.

5 Repeat steps 3 and 4 until you have sewn all the pieces together across the valance or curtain width. If there are any **half widths**, sew them onto an end. Press all of the seam allowances to one side.

6 Place the valance or curtain facedown on an ironing surface. **Press under (p. 198)** the lower edge 4" (10 cm), for the hem.

7 Unfold the pressed edge. Turn the cut edge back, aligning it to the pressed foldline; press the outer fold.

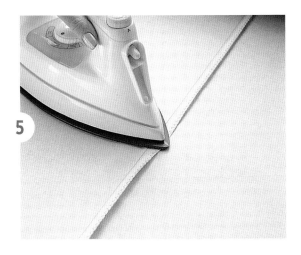

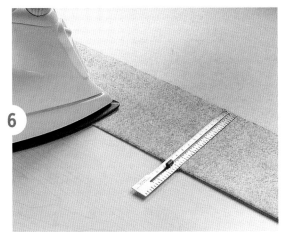

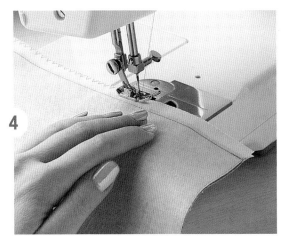

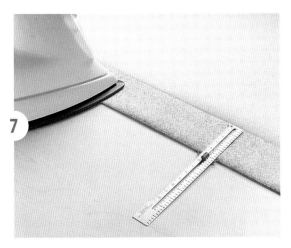

8 Refold the hem along the pressed foldlines, encasing the raw edge to form a 2" (5 cm) *double-fold hem (p. 98)*. Pin the hem, inserting the pins perpendicular to the foldlines.

9 Place the hem under the presser foot of the machine, with the wrong side of the valance or curtain facing up. The bulk of the fabric is positioned to the left of the machine. The side edge should be even with the back of the presser foot, with the needle aligned to enter the fabric just inside the inner fold.

10 Stitch the hem along the inner fold, backstitching at the beginning and the end about ½" (1.3 cm). Remove pins as you come to them.

TIP Double-fold side hems measure a total of 2" (5 cm): 1" (2.5 cm) turned under twice. Double-fold bottom hems on valances measure a total of 4" (10 cm): 2" (5 cm) turned under twice. Double-fold bottom hems on curtains measure a total of 8" (20.5 cm): 4" (10 cm) turned under twice.

QUICK REFERENCE

Half widths are always added at the outer edge of a valance or curtain panel. The seam is sewn along the edge that had the selvage; the side hem is sewn along the edge that was the center of the fabric width. (This is the only way you are able to match the pattern, if there is one.) Also, half panels go on the side of the treatment nearest the return.

How to Sew a Rod-pocket Treatment *continued*

11 Repeat steps 6 to 10 for the side hems, pressing under 2" (5 cm) first, instead of 4" (10 cm).

12 Press under ½" (1.3 cm) along the upper edge. Then, measuring from the pressed foldline, press under an amount equal to the heading height plus the rod-pocket depth. (Check your chart.) Insert pins along the lower foldline.

13 Place the folded upper edge under the presser foot of the machine, with the wrong side of the valance or curtain facing up. The bulk of the fabric is positioned to the left of the machine. The side hem should be even with the back of the presser foot, with the needle aligned to enter the fabric along the lower fold.

14 Stitch along the lower fold, across the entire width; backstitch about ½" (1.3 cm) at the beginning and the end. Remove pins as you come to them. This stitching line is the bottom of the rod pocket.

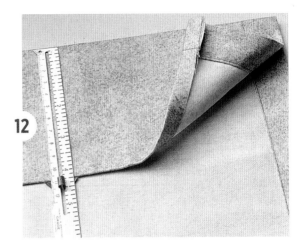

12

13

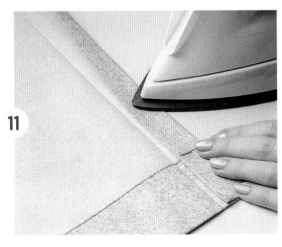

11

14

15 Measure the heading height, measuring on the wrong side, from the upper fold. Mark the stitching line, using chalk or an erasable marking pen. Pin frequently through both layers along the stitching line, inserting pins perpendicular to the line.

16 Stitch along the marked line across the entire width; backstitch at the beginning and end of the line. Remove pins as you come to them. This stitching line is the top of the rod pocket.

17 Press the valance or curtain one more time. Insert the rod into the rod pocket. Mount the rod on the brackets, following the instructions that came with the rod. Distribute the fullness evenly along the rod.

TIP Tape a small plastic bag over the end of the rod to make it slide more easily into the rod pocket.

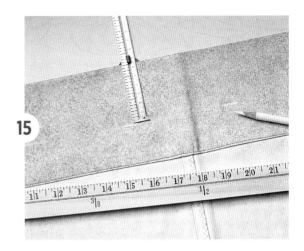

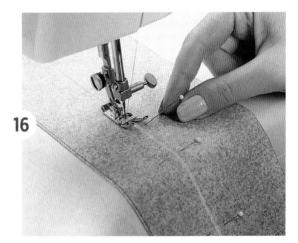

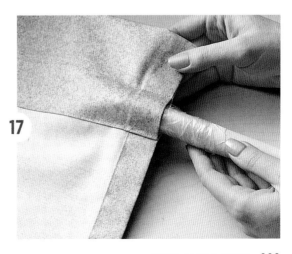

Rod-pocket Variations

Using this basic information about rod-pocket window fashions, you can make any of the styles shown on these pages.

Straight side panels are sewn with two times fullness and given a 3" (7.5 cm) heading. They are mounted on a wooden pole with elbows that have a 5" (12.5 cm) projection.

Café curtains and valances, mounted on standard curtain rods, have a 1½" (3.8 cm) heading depth and two times fullness.

Single panel drawn to one side is sewn with three times fullness. The 16" (40.5 cm) heading falls forward over a standard curtain rod to form an attached valance.

Floor-length sheers are made from railroaded lace fabric and mounted on a standard curtain rod. They are sewn with two-and-one-half times fullness and a 2½" (6.5 cm) heading.

Grommet Curtains

This easy-to-sew unlined curtain boasts an unexpected design feature: grommets. Surely no one will suspect you made them yourself, with such a high-tech look. Yet the grommets and the proper fastening tools are readily available at fabric stores, and they are surprisingly easy to use. Because this involves cutting holes in your curtain panel, always test the technique first on a sample of your fabric folded to the same thickness as the finished curtain!

Use one full width of fabric for each curtain panel. For best results, select lightweight to mediumweight fabric. This is a great opportunity to use an eye-catching decorative rod, since the curtain style is relatively simple.

WHAT YOU'LL LEARN . . . .

- How to install grommets
- How to use drapery weights (page 216)
- How to minimize bulk in multiple fabric layers

WHAT YOU'LL NEED . . . .

- Decorator fabric
- Thread to match
- Grommets, size 0, or
- ¼" (6 mm), and attaching tool kit
- Decorative rod and
- S-hooks
- Drapery weights

How to Sew a Grommet Curtain

1 Mount the rod so the bottom of the hooks will be above the window frame. Calculate the length of fabric needed for your curtain, working with the formula shown below. (We used these numbers for our curtain opposite; your numbers will probably be different.)

(continued)

Finished length, measured from ½" (1.3 cm) above the bottom of the hooks to the bottom of the treatment:	48" (122 cm)
Add the total bottom hem depth	+ 8" (20.5 cm)
Add 3" for the total upper hem	+ 3" (7.5 cm)
to find the cut length of each piece	= 59" (149.8 cm)

1

If your treatment has two curtain panels, multiply the cut length of each	59" (149.8 cm)
piece by 2	× 2
to find the length to buy	= 118"
	= 3 yd. 10" (3 m)

Purchase the next largest amount possible. If you buy a fabric with a pattern repeat, follow the chart until you have determined the cut length (59" [149.8 cm]). Your actual cut length must be rounded up to the next number evenly divisible by the pattern repeat. Proceed with the chart using this revised cut length measurement.

How to Sew a Grommet Curtain continued

2 Preshrink your fabric (page 41). Measure and mark the location of each cut along the selvage. Cut the curtain pieces, following the cutting guidelines on page 42. Cut away the selvages, cutting just beyond the tightly woven area.

3 Place the curtain facedown on a pressing surface. **Press under (p. 198)** the lower edge 8" (20.5 cm) for the hem. Unfold the pressed edge. Turn the cut edge back, aligning it to the pressed foldline; press the outer fold.

4 Refold the hem along the pressed foldlines, encasing the raw edge to form a 4" (5 cm) **double-fold hem (p. 98)**. Pin the hem, **inserting the pins perpendicular to the foldlines (p. 19)**.

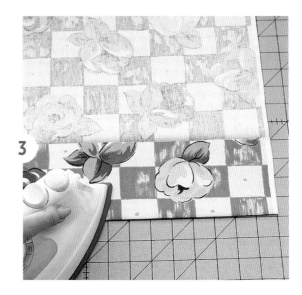

5 Place the hem under the presser foot of the machine, with the wrong side of the curtain facing up. The bulk of the fabric is positioned to the left of the machine. The side edge of the curtain should be even with the back of the presser foot, with the needle aligned to enter the fabric just inside the inner fold.

6 Stitch the hem along the inner fold, **back-stitching (p. 19)** a few stitches at the beginning and end. **Remove pins as you come to them (p. 19)**.

7 Repeat steps 3 to 6 for the side hems, pressing under 3" (7.5 cm) first, instead of 8" (20.5 cm). **Insert drapery weights** into the space between the layers of the lower hem before refolding the side hems.

TIP When you stitch past the drapery weight, half of the presser foot will probably travel over the weight. Place another weight under the presser foot on the opposite side to help you guide the fabric and keep your stitches even.

(continued)

QUICK REFERENCE

Insert drapery weights. Drapery weights make your curtains hang better at the sides, by pulling gently and constantly on the side hems. Inserted between the layers of the bottom hem, they are "trapped" in place when you stitch the side hem. Because they are made of metal, avoid hitting them with the needle.

How to Sew a Grommet Curtain *continued*

8 Repeat step 3 for the top hem, pressing under 3" (7.5 cm) first, instead of 8" (20.5 cm). Unfold the fabric at the corners. **Trim out excess fabric** from the inner layer, as shown, trimming to within ⅜" (1 cm) of the fold.

9 Refold the upper edge, and pin. Stitch along the inner fold, backstitching a few stitches at the beginning and end. Remove pins as you come to them.

10 Mark the placement for the grommets along the top hem, placing the end marks ¾" (2 cm) from the sides. Space the remaining marks evenly 6" to 10" (15 to 25.5 cm) apart.

TIP Closer spacing provides a more controlled upper edge, and consequently, a more even lower hem. When the grommets are spaced farther apart, the upper edge is allowed to droop gently between grommets and the lower hem will appear more uneven. To discover which look you prefer, hang your curtain panel, using safety pins, at various spacing patterns.

11 Read the manufacturer's directions for attaching the grommets, and test the technique on a sample. Attach the grommets at the marks, centering them between the fold and the stitching line of the top hem.

12 Insert decorative S-hooks through the grommets, and hang the curtain from the rod. Distribute the fullness evenly, and arrange the upper edge as desired between the hooks.

QUICK REFERENCE

Trim out excess fabric. Eliminating some of the bulk from this area will make it easier to install the end grommets. The cutting tool will have to go through only six layers of fabric, instead of nine.

Expanding the Idea

For a more decorative look, or if you don't care to
use grommets, substitute clip-on or sew-on hooks.

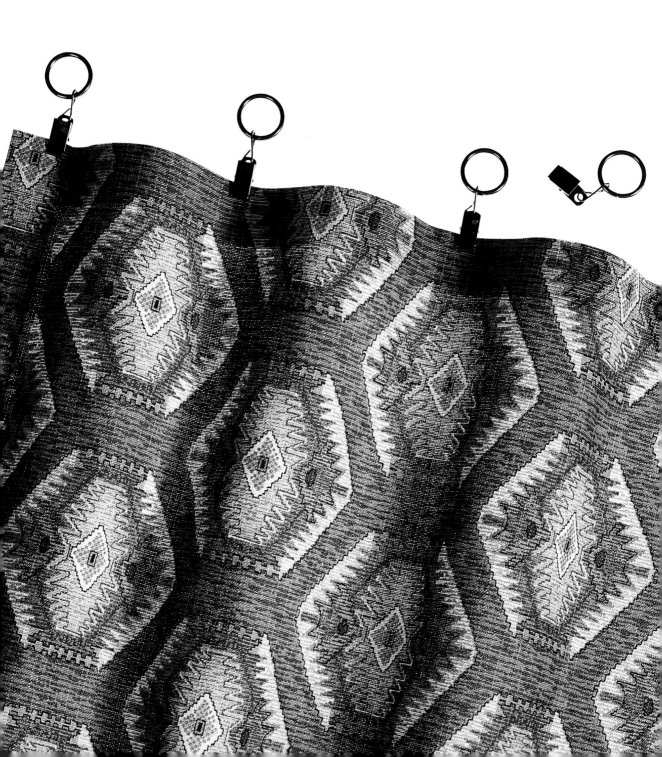

Glossary

Baste. Long, easy-to-remove stitches are sewn into the fabric temporarily, either by hand or by machine. Hand-basting stitches are used to hold layers of fabric and batting together for quilting. They are also used to gather a section of fabric into a smaller space. Machine-basting stitches are used to close a seam before inserting a zipper.

Bias. Any diagonal line intersecting the lengthwise and crosswise grains of fabric is referred to as bias. While woven fabric does not stretch on the lengthwise and crosswise grains, it has considerable stretch on the bias.

Casing. A fabric tunnel is sewn into the garment, often at the waistline, to carry elastic or cording.

Clip. Small, closely spaced cuts are made into the seam allowances of a garment or other project, usually along a curve or into a corner. When the item is turned right side out, the seam allowances can spread apart and lie flat where they have been clipped. Small clips are also used for marking the location of notches or dots from the pattern.

Courses. Corresponding to the crosswise grain of a woven fabric, the courses of a knit fabric run perpendicular to the selvages and ribs. Knit fabrics are most stretchy in the direction of the courses.

Crosswise grain. On woven fabric, the crosswise grain runs perpendicular to the selvages. Fabric has slight "give" in the crosswise grain.

Cut length refers to the total length at which fabric should be cut for a project. It includes allowances for hems, seams, matching any prints, and, for Roman shades, additional length for mounting.

Cut width refers to the total width at which fabric should be cut for a project. If more than one width of fabric (selvage to selvage) is needed, the cut width refers to the entire panel after seams are sewn, including allowances for any side hems or seams.

Drop length is the length of a tablecloth from the edge of the table to the edge of the cloth. It can be anywhere from 6" (15 cm) to floor-length.

Drop-shoulder. This garment design feature means that the seam joining the sleeve to the front and back is intended to fall down off the edge of the shoulder, rather than align to the shoulder crest. Drop-shoulder styles are rather relaxed, less fitted, and generally have more room in the armhole.

Ease. Some fabric length, beyond what you have calculated, will be "eaten up" by turning under and stitching any double-fold hems, heading, or rod pocket. Also, when a treatment is gathered onto a rod, the length may "shrink up" a bit. By adding ½" (1.3 cm) to the length before cutting, your finished length will be more accurate.

Edgestitch. With the machine set for straight stitching at a length of 2 to 2.5 mm or 10 stitches per inch, stitch within ⅛" (3 mm) of a finished edge. With many machines, this can be achieved by guiding the inner edge of the right presser foot toe along the outer finished edge.

Facing. A fabric extension or addition that is sewn as a backing to another piece protects raw edges or seam allowances from raveling and gives the item a neat, finished appearance. For instance, a jacket front and neckline have an outer layer and an underlayer, or facing.

Finished length refers to the total length of a project after it is sewn. For a tablecloth, this includes the table length and twice the drop length; for a Roman shade, finished length is measured from the top of the mounting board to the window sill or apron.

Finished width refers to the total width of a project after it is sewn. For a tablecloth, this includes the table width plus twice the drop length. For an inside-mounted Roman shade, the finished width is the inside width of the window frame; for an outside-mounted shade, the finished width includes the window frame width plus 1" (2.5 cm) beyond the frame on both sides.

Fullness describes the finished width of the curtain or valance in proportion to the length of the rod or mounting board. For example, two times fullness means that the width of the curtain measures two times the length of the rod.

Gather. Two rows of long machine stitches are sewn along a seamline. When the bobbin threads are pulled, the fabric slides along the stitches into tiny tucks. Gathers are used to fit a wide garment section to a narrower section while at the same time adding shaping.

Grading. Seam allowances on faced edges are trimmed to graduated widths to eliminate a bulky ridge. Often the garment seam allowance is trimmed to ¼" (6 mm) and the facing seam allowance is trimmed to ⅛" (3 mm).

Heading is the portion at the top of a rod-pocket window treatment that forms a ruffle when the curtain is on the rod. The depth of the heading is the distance from the finished upper edge to the top stitching line for the rod pocket.

Hemming. The outer edge of a project is given a neat finished appearance by turning under and securing the raw edge in one of several methods. It may be turned under twice and stitched, encasing the raw edge, as for the side and bottom hems of a curtain panel. It may be turned under once and fused in place, as for the Roman shade. The round tablecloth is hemmed by stitching welting or bias tape to the outer edge.

Inside mount refers to a window treatment that is installed inside the window frame.

Lengthwise grain. On woven fabric, the lengthwise grain runs parallel to the selvages. Fabrics are generally stronger and more stable along the lengthwise grain.

Lined to the edge means that a fabric panel is backed with lining that is cut to the exact same size. The two pieces are joined together by a seam around the outer edge; the seam allowances are encased between the layers.

Lining is a fabric backing sewn to the top fabric to provide extra body, protection from sunlight, and support for outer hems or seams.

Mark. It is often necessary to give yourself temporary guidelines or guide points on the fabric for cutting, stitching, or matching seams. There are many tools and methods for doing this, such as marking pencils and pens, chalk dispensers, tape, or pins.

Miter. Excess fabric is folded out at an angle to eliminate bulk. You probably miter the corners when you wrap gifts.

Nap. Some fabrics have definite "up" and "down" directions, either because of a surface pile, like corduroy or velveteen, or because of a one-way print. When laying out a pattern on napped fabric, cut all the pieces with the top edges facing the same direction.

Nominal lumber. The actual measurement of nominal or "stock" lumber differs from the nominal measurement. A 1 × 2 board actually measures ¾" × 1½" (2 × 3.8 cm); a 1 × 4 board measures ¾" × 3½" (2 × 9 cm). Be sure to measure the board for accuracy.

Nondirectional print. The design printed on this fabric has no definite "up" and "down" directions, and pattern pieces can be laid out with the top edges facing in either direction.

Outside mount refers to any window treatment that is installed on the wall above and to the side of the window frame.

Patch pockets. One of the easiest pocket styles to sew, these are sewn to the outer surface of the garment like a "patch."

Pattern repeat, a characteristic of decorator fabrics, is the lengthwise distance from one distinctive point in the pattern, such as the tip of a petal in a floral pattern, to the exact same point in the next pattern design.

Pivot. Perfect corners are stitched by stopping with the needle down in the fabric at the exact corner before turning. To be sure the corner stitch locks, turn the handwheel until the needle goes all the way down and just begins to rise. Then raise the presser foot, turn the fabric, lower the presser foot, and continue stitching.

Preshrink. Fabric that shrinks, especially natural fibers, shrinks most in the first laundering. If you intend to launder your finished item occasionally, you should wash the fabric before cutting out the pieces, so the item will not shrink after you make it. "Dry clean only" fabrics can be preshrunk by steaming them with your iron.

Press. This step is extremely important to the success of your sewing projects. Select the heat setting appropriate for your fabric, and use steam. Lift and lower the iron in an overlapping pattern. Do not slide the iron down the seam, as this can cause the fabric to stretch out of shape, especially on the crosswise grain or bias.

Projection is the distance a rod or mounting board stands out from the wall.

Railroading. The lengthwise grain of the fabric is run horizontally in the window treatment, eliminating the need for any vertical seams. Some decorator fabrics are intentionally made this way, in widths that can accommodate floor-length treatments.

Return is the portion of the curtain or top treatment extending from the end of the rod or mounting board to the wall, blocking the side light and view.

Ribbing is a very stretchy knit fabric, usually with pronounced ridges. It is especially suitable for necks and cuffs on knit garments, since it can easily stretch to go over heads and hands, yet spring back in shape once in place. Most ribbing comes in much narrower widths than other fabrics and, because you use less of it, it is often sold by the inch (centimeter) rather than the yard (meter).

Ribs. Corresponding to the lengthwise grain in woven fabric, the ribs of a knit fabric run parallel to the selvages (if there are any). Knits are usually most stable in the rib direction.

Rod pocket is a stitched fabric tunnel in a curtain where the curtain rod or pole is inserted. Stitching lines at the top and bottom of the pocket keep the rod or pole in place.

Rotary cutter and mat. These time-saving tools for cutting fabric may also take a little practice and serious precautions. The blade on a rotary cutter is extremely sharp. Cut slowly, watch your fingers, and always retract or cover the blade between cuts. The rotary cutter cannot be used without the special protective mat.

Seam. Two pieces of fabric are placed right sides together and joined along the edge with stitches. After stitching, the raw edges are hidden on the wrong side, leaving a clean, smooth line on the right side.

Seam allowance. Narrow excess fabric lies between the stitching line and the raw edges. The standard seam allowance width for garment sewing is ⅝" (1.5 cm); the standard width for home décor sewing is ½" (1.3 cm). The seam allowance gives the seam strength and ensures that the stitches cannot be pulled off the raw edges.

Seam ripper. It doesn't really rip. Use the sharp point to slide under and cut stitches one at a time. Avoid the temptation to simply slide the cutting hook down the seam. You will inevitably cut into your fabric. Even the most experienced sewers rely on their seam rippers.

Selvages. Characteristic of woven fabrics, this narrow, tightly woven outer edge should be cut away. Avoid the temptation to use it as one side of a cut piece, as it may cause the seam to pucker and may shrink excessively when laundered. One exception to this rule is sewing long vertical seams on sheer or loosely woven curtains, where trimming the selvages off could cause excessive raveling. In this case, leave the selvages intact and clip into them every 1" (2.5 cm) to allow them to relax.

Separating zipper. Zippers that come completely apart at the bottom are intended for use in items like jackets or the tote on page 149. Check the label carefully in the store, to be sure you are buying the correct zipper style.

Tacking. Short stationary stitches, sewn by hand or by machine, hold two or more pieces of fabric together a little less conspicuously then a row of stitches.

Thread jam. The threads become tangled up in a wad on the underside of the fabric and the machine gets "stuck." The best way to prevent a thread jam is to hold both top and bottom thread tails to the back or side of the presser foot until completing the first few stitches of a seam. If a thread jam happens, DON'T USE FORCE! Remove the presser foot, if you can. Snip all the threads you can get at from the top of the throat plate. Open the bobbin case door or throat plate, and snip any threads you can get at. Remove the bobbin, if you can. Gently remove the fabric. Thoroughly clean out the feed dog and bobbin area before reinserting the bobbin and starting over.

Topstitching is a decorative and functional stitching line placed ¼" to 1" (6 mm to 2.5 cm) from the finished edge of an item. The stitching is done with the right side of the item facing up. Sometimes topstitching is done with a heavier thread or two threads through the machine needle, to make it more visible.

Understitching is straight stitching very close to the seamline that connects a facing to the garment. After the seam allowances are trimmed, clipped, and pressed toward the facing, stitch from the right side of the facing to keep it from rolling to the outside of the garment.

Index